Reason and Reverence

Reason and Reverence

Religious Humanism for the 21st Century

William R. Murry

SKINNER HOUSE BOOKS

BOSTON

Printed in the United States.

ISBN 1-55896-518-1
978-1-55896-518-8

10 9 8 7 6 5 4 3
09 08

Library of Congress Cataloging-in-Publication Data

Murry, William R.
  Reason and reverence : religious humanism for the 21st century / by
William R. Murry.
     p. cm.
  Includes bibliographical references and index.
  ISBN-13: 978-1-55896-518-8 (pbk. : alk. paper)
  ISBN-10: 1-55896-518-1 (pbk. : alk. paper) 1. Humanism, Religious.
2. Unitarian Universalist Association—Doctrines. I. Title.
  BX9841.3.M87 2006
  211'.6—dc22
                              2006016875

Skinner House Books and the Unitarian Universalist Association of Congregations are committed to the use of gender-inclusive language. For the purposes of historical accuracy, however, quoted material has been printed as originally written.

To Barbara
sine qua non

A religion, old or new, that stressed the magnificence of the universe as revealed by modern science, might be able to draw forth reserves of reverence and awe hardly tapped by the conventional faiths. Sooner or later, such a religion will emerge.

Carl Sagan

Contents

Foreword

RELIGION is serious business. Unfortunately, we often find it treated in today's culture as part of the entertainment industry, or as a social organization like the Kiwanis or the Lions Club, a vaguely benevolent force for social good. Religion can too easily become nothing more than a substitute for organic community, a haven in an otherwise alienating world.

Events in the twenty-first century have conspired to remind us that religion is indeed serious, even hazardous. Incredible pain and suffering have been inflicted in its name. As global terrorism and the emerging theocratic tendencies in our own nation show us, there is virtually no policy that cannot find some religious justification somewhere. As Sophia Lyon Fahs insists, "It matters what we believe." What we believe shapes what we shall become and what we will accept.

In this book, my friend and colleague Bill Murry invites those of us who have thought of ourselves as religious humanists or who have been intrigued by religious humanism to explore the underlying assumptions of that vision. With a deep appreciation for the religious and intellectual history in which we are rooted, Dr. Murry calls us to an honest and open evaluation of the strengths and weaknesses of traditional religious humanism. In exploring its rich and often neglected potential, he argues that an enlarged humanism is able to engage the issues and needs of our times with honesty and integrity. He challenges us to recognize the self-imposed limitations that have prevented humanists from fully engaging the spiritual yearnings of contemporary society and have thus muted the humanist witness.

What emerges from Murry's exploration is a vision of religious humanism that embraces both reason and reverence, that celebrates human embeddedness in a natural world that is everywhere sacred, that affirms the essential unity of all who are engaged in the ongoing human venture, that encourages us to live richly with dark realities, that seeks justice and marries justice to mercy. In this age of fundamentalisms, Murry urges religious humanism as a guard against the dangerous potential of religious conviction—its too frequent willingness to ratify madness and murder and to prioritize unexamined assumptions over compassion.

Acutely aware of the profound dangers that confront the human venture at every turn, Murry invites us to explore the humanist alternative in relation to the ever-present and constantly growing ecological challenge that threatens the very existence of human civilization, persistent and pernicious social problems like poverty and racism, and constant pressure to surrender freedom in the name of security. Murry believes that religious humanism has an important message for our times and that religious humanists have an obligation to find the language that will allow that message to be heard.

The history of religion is so soaked in blood that we might be well advised to shake ourselves free from its claims. However, human history would suggest that we are hard-wired to be religious. Human beings seem to be religious animals by nature. Even those of us who reject traditional theist religion do so religiously. We seem to be driven by a need to relate our quotidian existence to cosmic concepts, to find in the events of daily life some hint of eternal significance. So it is important that we be as intentional as possible in our religious expression, so that we can examine and understand the function of religion in our lives.

Murry invites us to be consciously intentional about the humanist alternative in religion—to understand its strengths and weaknesses, to find a language that will allow us to engage the religious conversation of our time, to find the larger dimension of life that will allow us to bring moral and ethical judgments to bear on the issues of the day, to embrace the larger vision that will allow us to live lives of purpose and direction. In times like these, we cannot afford business as usual. It is critical that we accept the invitation this volume offers to explore who we are as religious humanists, whence we have come, whither we are tending, and what, in an increasingly chaotic world, we can say and do that truly matters.

David E. Bumbaugh
Professor of Ministry
Meadville Lombard Theological School

Introduction

IN 1933 the signers of the first Humanist Manifesto proclaimed, "Any religion that can hope to be a synthesizing and dynamic force for today must be shaped to the needs of this age." More than seventy years later, that same understanding is the basis for this book. The Manifesto's signers were attempting to introduce to the world a new kind of religion, one that left the myths, symbols, and rituals of traditional religion behind while providing a foundation for morality and meaning grounded in human reason.

The Manifesto succeeded beautifully in articulating a vital new religious perspective for the time in which it was written. It rejected the idea of a supernatural deity, held that the natural universe is all there is, and regarded human beings as a part of nature. Affirming the intrinsic value of all human beings, it maintained the realization of human potential in the here and now as the goal of human life and social justice as necessary to achieve that goal. It understood the religious dimension to include all of life but believed it was especially manifested "in a heightened sense of personal life and in a cooperative effort to promote social well-being."

As the years passed and times changed, however, the weaknesses and limitations of religious humanism became apparent. New cultural movements such as feminism and postmodernism transformed the American psyche, and the horrors of the Holocaust and the

Soviet Gulag cast serious doubt on the optimistic view of human nature held by the early humanists. In addition, concerns about the environment, not apparent in 1933, became critical for human survival as well as the quality of life. And finally, what had begun as a dynamic religious vision gradually became petrified for many into a dogmatic rationalism.

The subsequent Manifestos of 1973 and 2003 addressed some of these issues, but it seemed to me that the time had come for a more comprehensive treatment of religious humanism, one that addressed in greater depth the changes needed for humanism to be "shaped to the needs of this age." This book both defends humanism against its detractors and describes my vision of a new humanism, one that offers depth, meaning, and purpose without sacrificing intellectual honesty or the spiritual dimension. Religious humanism is a life stance that exults in being alive in this unimaginably vast and breathtakingly beautiful universe and that finds joy and satisfaction in contributing to human betterment. Without a creed but with an emphasis on reason, compassion, community, nature, and social responsibility, it is a way of living that answers the religious and spiritual needs of people today. The emerging religious humanism is informed by cultural developments and recent discoveries in the natural and human sciences and grounded in the larger context of religious naturalism.

Religious naturalism is a perspective that finds religious meaning in the natural world and rejects the notion of a supernatural realm. It has a long tradition dating back at least to the philosopher Spinoza. In recent years, religious naturalism has been enjoying a resurgence. Most religious naturalists are theists who understand God as belonging to the natural universe rather than as a supernatural deity. This book describes a non-theistic form, a perspective that I call *humanistic religious naturalism*. In one sense, this would seem to be no different from traditional religious humanism, which rejects the supernatural and maintains that there is only one reality, the natural universe. However, traditional humanism has historically been too anthropocentric;

whereas for humanistic religious naturalism, nature rather than humankind is ultimate. This lays the foundation for a strong environmental ethic, a necessity in a world threatened by environmental destruction. Further, integrating religious humanism with religious naturalism results in a greater spiritual depth and a language of reverence, both of which many find missing in traditional religious humanism. This emergent form of humanism also provides a meaningful story, the epic of evolution. The differences with traditional religious humanism may seem subtle, but they provide a foundation for a more open and inclusive humanism that speaks to the heart and the soul, not just the intellect.

At the same time, naturalism is not a sufficient source of religious meaning because nature is morally neutral or simply amoral. Its only value would seem to be creativity. Nature has produced what we perceive as the magnificence of the universe. Through evolution it created humankind, who in turn developed moral principles. But nature's rain falls on the just and the unjust. Disease and death afflict everyone, regardless of character. Nature knows nothing of justice, love, kindness, or generosity. Humanism, with its conviction of the dignity and value of all humans and all that follows from this principle, provides the values that naturalism lacks.

Moreover, it seems to me that religious naturalism, in either its theistic or nontheistic form, is the basic theological perspective of liberal religion, particularly of Unitarian Universalism. The study *Engaging Our Theological Diversity*, by the Commission on Appraisal of the Unitarian Universalist Association, reinforces this conviction in several ways. The Commission's survey revealed that the seventh Principle, affirming "respect for the interdependent web of all existence" is "at the center of our shared worldview" and that most respondents reject the idea of a two-story universe consisting of the natural and the supernatural. Further, most respondents who referred to God as part of their theology spoke of God in naturalistic terms as the power of creativity, an immanent force for good in the world, or simply as mystery. In a word, finding the sacred in the natural world appears to be one of the major characteristics of religious liberalism. This rejection of supernaturalism distinguishes liberal religion from other forms of Western religion.

Since humanistic religious naturalism represents a merger of two traditions, religious humanism and religious naturalism, parts of the book deal primarily with one tradition or the other, and some sections deal with the fusion of the two. In order to describe a culture we have to discuss each of its constituent parts—art, literature, religion, politics, economics—yet what we are describing is the larger culture. Similarly it is necessary to understand humanistic religious naturalism by dealing, sometimes separately, with its constituent parts, the two traditions it merges.

Scholars often differentiate between two kinds of religion, *mythos* and *logos*. *Mythos* refers to imaginative religion based on myths, or stories with meanings. Myths provide an explanation of why things are the way they are and give a deeper meaning to life. The two creation stories in the Hebrew Bible are among the most famous myths in Western culture. I believe that myths were never meant to be taken literally but were probably understood even by a pre-scientific people as metaphorical attempts to describe a reality that was too complex and mysterious to comprehend in any other way. It is only in a scientific age, with its emphasis on factual knowledge, that myths have come to be understood as facts. By taking myths literally, fundamentalist religion replaces *mythos* with *logos*.

Logos is rational religion, which in our time usually means religion based on the scientific-empirical worldview. Rational religion developed primarily in Greek philosophy, much of which is essentially a rationalized version of Greek mythology. It also arose to some extent in the Hebrew prophets, who rebelled against rituals and ceremony and emphasized moral living and social justice. Humanistic religious naturalism is a contemporary form of *logos* religion.

Myths and stories are important to religion, for they speak to our subconscious minds and therefore affect us at a deep level and influence our basic assumptions and attitudes. Although humanistic religious naturalism belongs to the *logos* type of religion, it does have stories that serve the same function as myths in providing a narrative understanding of the origin and meaning of the universe and of human life. One of these is the story of cosmic and biological evolution. It is the story of the creative, emergent powers of nature, and that story continues today in the form of the moral, spiritual, social, and cultural evolution that human creativity is bringing about. A second story, one consistent with the values of humanism, is the remarkable history of the expansion of human freedom in the world, both religious and political freedom.

Humanism has long been a target of the religious right. Several years ago the Reverend Tim LaHaye proclaimed, "Humanists are the mortal enemy of all pro-moral Americans, and the most serious threat to our nation in its entire history." LaHaye is a leading evangelical Christian minister and co-author of the *Left Behind* series. LaHaye, Jerry Falwell, and others have blamed humanism for everything they believe to be wrong with America, such as reproductive choice, anti-poverty programs, the feminist movement, the gay rights movement, laws against compulsory prayer in public schools, gun control, and sexuality education.

They are both right and wrong. They are dead wrong in calling humanists a threat to the nation's morality, for humanism is a highly ethical way of life, but they are right in giving humanists credit for bringing about social change. I believe that the kind of religious humanism described in this book offers the finest, most helpful, and most honest convictions and values available. It also offers a critique of previous articulations of humanism.

This book does not pretend to speak for others. By articulating my understanding of the emerging humanism, I hope to help readers see it as a viable option for today's world. In her monumental study, *A History of God*, Karen Armstrong writes,

> When religious ideas have lost their validity, they have usually faded away painlessly; if the human idea of God no longer works for us in the empirical age, it will be discarded.

Yet in the past people have always created new symbols to act as a focus for spirituality. Human beings have always created a faith for themselves, to cultivate their sense of the wonder and ineffable significance of life.

In this empirical age, humanistic religious naturalism can and should be that faith.

Why I Am a Religious Humanist

SOME TIME AGO a neighbor, upon learning that I was a humanist, asked me what that meant. I replied that humanism refers to the affirmation of the worth and dignity of every person, a commitment to human betterment, and the necessity for human beings to take responsibility for themselves and the world. "Sounds like I'm a humanist, too," he replied, seeming surprised. In this broad meaning of humanism, millions of people are humanists who do not identify as such, and humanist values permeate our cultural institutions.

I explained to my neighbor that there are many kinds of humanism, each with a different adjective to denote its particularity, including Christian humanism, Jewish humanism, existentialist humanism, secular humanism, and religious humanism. I further explained that some of these are theistic, whereas religious humanism and its cousin, secular humanism, are nontheistic. When I write of humanism, I mean it in its nontheistic sense.

I also suggested that, while secular and religious humanism agree on many tenets, religious humanism emphasizes the importance of communities that affirm, support, and encourage these values through preaching, teaching, caring for one another, and celebrating life and life's passages together. Secular humanism does not for the most part. Moreover, I said, religious humanism has a different feel or quality than secular humanism because it is more open to mystery and more likely to respond with reverence and gratitude at the wonder of being alive.

Religious humanism affirms the intrinsic value of every human being; it maintains that all persons are ends in themselves and not means to another's ends. It holds that we humans make our lives meaningful through personal and spiritual growth and by optimizing the good and opposing that which is evil. It emphasizes personal freedom and the application of critical thinking and natural intelligence in making choices and guiding one's actions. It places a high priority on democracy as a political philosophy and a way of organizing society for the wellbeing of all, and it is committed to justice and equity for every person. Religious humanism is devoted to learning and to increasing knowledge, especially through the use of reason and the scientific-empirical method. It emphasizes life in the here and now and does not expect another life after death. It upholds intellectual honesty and rejects superstition. Since it denies the supernatural, it insists that we can rely only on ourselves to establish a better world. It is optimistic about the future, although this optimism is tempered by the understanding that humans too often pursue their own interests at the expense of the common good. And religious humanism finds great value in human beings coming together in religious community to deepen their understanding, support and strengthen their values, celebrate life's passages, and work together for a better world.

I have not always been a humanist. I was brought up as a Southern Baptist Christian. I was even ordained by my Southern Baptist church, although I nearly flunked the ordination examination because I did not believe in the virgin birth and would not lie about it. That was considered heresy, since it was thought to throw doubt on the divinity of Jesus. The church deacons at the examination—men who had known me since I was a child—voted for me. Most of the ministers voted against me, then walked out when they lost and did not participate in the ordination. I knew then that I would never be a Southern Baptist minister.

The more I learned about the origins of religion and the way the Bible was written, and the more I studied psychology, philosophy, and world religions, the more religiously liberal I became, until I realized that I had become a humanist. My story is not unique.

In particular my skepticism began with the study of modern biblical scholarship and with a college course I taught that dealt with the religious theories of Marx, Feuerbach, Freud, and Nietzsche. Another course I taught, dealing with modern literature and religious faith, included works by Dostoevsky, Melville, Sartre, and Camus that reinforced my skeptical tendencies, especially because of their treatment of the prevalence of evil in the world despite the presence of an all-powerful, loving God. My study of modern theology, especially the thought of Paul Tillich and the process theologians, increased my doubts. I gradually gave up belief in a supernatural deity. The four issues that made it the most difficult for me to sustain my belief in a loving God were moral, epistemological, psychological, and sociopolitical.

The Moral Problem

The question is ages old and perplexing: Why does God, who is supposed to be both perfectly good and all-powerful, allow innocent people to suffer and die and permit many other kinds of terrible injustices?

At one point in Dostoevsky's novel *The Brothers Karamazov*, Ivan Karamazov relates several incidents of brutality against little children, and he expresses his outrage at a God who allows such unjust and unnecessary suffering. "I must have justice," he says, "not justice in some remote infinite time and space, but here on earth, and that I could see myself." If the suffering of little children is necessary to pay for the harmony of the world or to pay for truth, then Ivan believes the price is too high. He cannot accept a God who allows children to be tortured, nor can he love a world in which innocent children suffer and die.

Camus' Dr. Rieux, the hero of *The Plague*, uses similar words. Bubonic plague has struck Oran, where Rieux lives, and he treats hundreds of patients but loses almost all of them. After he and a priest have worked side by side in a vain attempt to save a little boy, they engage in a brief conversation. The priest suggests that we have to learn to accept death, and we must love what we cannot understand. Dr. Rieux replies, "No, Father, I've a very different idea of love. And until my dying day, I shall refuse to love a scheme of things in which little children are put to torture."

These two books had a profound effect on me, as did Elie Wiesel's little book, *Night*, a powerful autobiographical depiction of life in a Nazi death camp. So did Rabbi Richard Rubenstein's *After Auschwitz*, in which a rabbi asks how one can believe in a God who did not prevent the brutal and inhuman deaths of six million Jews. This question has led a number of Jewish theologians and lay people alike out of theism and into humanism.

The untimely deaths of innocent children haunted my years as a parish minister—a beautiful little ten-year-old girl experiencing a slow, painful death from cancer, her face swollen and disfigured by the disease; a promising sixteen-year-old boy killed by his best friend as they played with an "unloaded" pistol; an infant born with a congenital heart defect, slowly dying despite several surgeries. I conducted their memorial services, but only after shedding many tears, and I could not reconcile these deaths with belief in a loving God.

It seems to me that either God is not perfectly good or God is not all-powerful. Either represents a repudiation of the traditional Western concept of God.

An early treatment of the problem is found in the book of Job in the Hebrew Bible. Job, who is described as a righteous, God-fearing, and decent man, suffers terribly. He loses his children, his riches, and his health, and he asks what he has done to deserve this. His presupposition is that a just, loving, and all-powerful God rewards goodness and punishes evil. The answer given to Job is twofold. First, suffering is not the result of evil acts being punished by God. Second, God's ways are beyond our understanding, and we should accept them even though we cannot comprehend their purpose. We are, after all, mortal and finite, and we must not expect to know why everything happens the way it does. Who are we to question the infinite?

These and other efforts to provide a reasonable answer within a theistic framework to the question of "why bad things happen to good people" were not satisfying to me.

The Epistemological Problem

I have grown to believe that we discover truth primarily through the scientific-empirical method, not through revelation, intuition, or extrasensory perception. I believe we have no knowledge other than that which begins with sensory experience, with what we see or hear or feel or taste or smell. We then are able to reason from our experience using both analytical and constructive thinking to form ideas and images, to draw conclusions, to construct arguments, and to generate plans, goals, and purposes. But we have no extrasensory perception of another world. Therefore I do not have any reason to believe in a supernatural being or a supernatural realm. As far as we can know, there is only the one natural universe of matter-energy. Philosophically, I am a naturalist; I believe that all that exists is part of the natural, inconceivably vast, and wonder-filled universe.

Closely related to scientific method are the discoveries of modern science and what they tell us about human life and the world. In particular, the theory of evolution by natural selection has had profound implications for religious belief, including mine. Some of the details of evolution may be debatable, but that human life descended from other forms of life seems undeniable, thanks to the immense body of scientific evidence. Evolutionary theory posits that human consciousness and the human mind are products of evolution. They are simply the highest functions of the one substance that exists, which I think of as matter-energy. Evolution means that human beings are not the product of a special creation, and as a part and product of nature, we cannot consist of an eternal spiritual substance temporarily imprisoned in a physical body.

Thus both the empirical method of modern science and the remarkable results of that method led me away from supernaturalism.

The Psychological Problem

I think Freud was right when he suggested that traditional religion is the result of the adult projecting onto the cosmic order the infant's dependence on the parent. That is, as human beings we feel the need for someone to depend on to help us get through the crises we face—the suffering, the grief and loss, and finally our own deaths. Just as the infant has seemingly almighty parents who provide for all his or her needs, so this longing for someone on whom we can depend lingers throughout our lives, and that is the role God plays in the lives of most people.

I also find the views of Ludwig Feuerbach in *The Essence of Christianity* to be persuasive. Feuerbach suggests that the idea of God is a projection of the best qualities, noblest values, and highest ideals humankind can imagine. Thus we humans created God in our own image, not vice versa as the Bible teaches. Feuerbach proposes that if birds had a god, it would be the perfect bird.

Similarly, John Dewey suggests that in Western religion, God represents the highest ideals of human beings—ideals to which we have ascribed material reality in the form of a supernatural, all-powerful, all-knowing, and all-seeing deity. The University of Chicago theologian G. B. Foster suggests an analogy between God and Uncle Sam: Just as Americans created Uncle Sam to personify their patriotic spirit and ideals, so ancient peoples created God as an anthropomorphized embodiment of their highest values.

I am also persuaded that religion arose out of early human beings' fears of the unknown and their need to have a supernatural parent to protect them from wild beasts, earthquakes, famine, floods, and other natural disasters. Beliefs can be true irrespective of our motivations for holding them, but the idea that human beings created God out of fear increases my skepticism.

Sociopolitical Problems

Religion is a powerful cultural force. As I look back through history and even at the world of today, I see damaging ripple effects of theistic, authoritarian belief systems. Authoritarian religions have disempowered people by mandating what they should think and what they should do and not do. As Freud and others have noted, this disempowerment has calcified people's minds and prevented critical thinking. Authoritarian theistic religions are usually intolerant of differences in religious beliefs and practices, and intolerance often leads to violence. From the burning of individual heretics to wars to acts of terrorism, world history is testimony to the horrors of religious absolutism. The Nazi extermination of the Jews was built on the foundation of the history of anti-Semitism in Europe, including the idea of Jews as the killers of Jesus.

Sharon Welch has noted that belief in an all-powerful deity leads to authoritarian institutions, including governments, because it glorifies domination. In her important book *The Feminist Ethic of Risk*, she explains,

> The idea of an omnipotent and sovereign God . . . assumes that absolute power can be a good. In the Christian tradition, one does not attribute demonic or destructive traits to Deity. And yet absolute power *is* a destructive trait. It assumes that the ability to act regardless of the response of others is a good rather than a sign of alienation from others.

A significant part of the authoritarian problem is the Western depiction of God as male, which is used to justify a patriarchal society that regards women as inferior in every way. In this country, women have been able to vote or hold political office for fewer than a hundred years, and we have yet to elect a woman president. Even today women are underrepresented in national political and business leadership and are underpaid compared with men in similar jobs. In Islamic countries, inequality is much worse. In both cultures, men are seen as participating in divinity in a way that women cannot. For centuries, neither churches nor synagogues ordained women to be ministers, priests, or rabbis, and of course, the Roman Catholic church and several conservative Christian groups still do not.

Religions that don't encourage questioning and independent thought are ill-suited as transformational forces in society. Many Christian churches simply reflect and reinforce the values of society, the status quo. Happily, some exceptions to this rule come to mind, especially the involvement of the churches in the civil rights movement under the leadership of Rev. Dr. Martin Luther King. But too often, churches have been complacent in the face of economic injustice, racism, sexism, homophobia, and militarism, instead of being in the forefront of the fight against these dehumanizing oppressions. The conservative churches are the worst in this regard, but even the more liberal Christian churches are complicit, as seen in numerous conflicts over the ordination of women or gay people.

The doctrine of original sin is another stumbling block for me. I believe it is often manifested in the practice of relying on prayer rather than hard work to accomplish valid goals. The famous phrase in the prayer of general confession in the Episcopal Book of Common Prayer, that "there is no health in us," illustrates an emphasis on innate human impotence and depravity and gives followers an excuse not to develop as human beings or fight for justice.

For all these reasons, I cannot accept the idea of a supernatural deity.

Alternative Concepts of God

I am aware, of course, of various efforts to redefine God in terms more acceptable to modern minds, especially those within the naturalistic tradition. For example, some conceive of God not as a supernatural being but as the driving force of the natural world;

not as all-powerful but as one whose power is the magnetic or persuasive power of love; and therefore not as a god who imposes his will or intervenes in human history. By limiting God's power while maintaining God's absolute goodness, these theologians posit a finite God struggling alongside humankind. Such a concept addresses the problem of how God allows suffering, but it does not resolve the other difficulties I have described.

Other thinkers have identified God as the universal self in each person or the power of creativity in the universe (e.g., Henry Nelson Wieman). Still others conceive of God as the power for good in the world and in every person, or simply as "the spirit" or the spirit of love. In these conceptions, God is no longer understood as the personal supernatural being of the Western religious traditions and of most lay believers today but as an apparently impersonal natural force. The transcendent God has become immanent; the supernatural God has become part of the natural world; the omnipotent God has become the power of good to attract. The question then becomes whether such a god has any real meaning and whether such a theology can be satisfying intellectually, ethically, or emotionally. It does not work for me, but there is a very fine line between this idea, called naturalistic theism, and what I call humanistic religious naturalism.

Some wish to retain the word *God* for devotional purposes. For example, the religious naturalist Jerome Stone, in his outstanding book, *The Minimalist Vision of Transcendence*, states that while he does not often use the word *God*, he can use it to refer to "the world perceived in its value-enhancing and value-attracting aspects." He can also say that "God is the sum total of the ecosystem, community and person empowering and demanding interactions in the universe."

These naturalistic concepts are efforts to save the idea of God, but to me they represent personifications of natural or human forces.

A possible refutation of my views comes from brain researchers Andrew Newberg and Eugene D'Aquili in their book, *Why God*

Won't Go Away, which claims that the religious impulse is hard-wired into the biology of the brain. Using a high-tech radioactive emission tool producing brain images of people in a deep meditative state, they have found "evidence of a neurological process that has evolved to allow us humans to transcend material existence and acknowledge and connect with a deeper, more spiritual part of ourselves perceived of as an absolute, universal reality that connects us to all that is." This occurs when the orientation area of the brain, the top-rear part of the cerebrum which enables us to distinguish between self and world, is deprived of sensory input. Then the individual feels a sense of oneness with God or the cosmos.

However, far from proving the reality of a supernatural deity, their research simply locates the place in the brain responsible for the mystic's feeling of oneness with all. The experience can be interpreted as being connected to a divine source or as simply being a sense of oneness with the natural world. One of their subjects, a non-theistic Buddhist, referred to the experience as "a sense of timelessness and infinity. It feels like I am part of everyone and everything in existence." How a person interprets the experience depends on the worldview he or she brings to the experience.

On the other hand, philosopher and religious naturalist Loyal Rue suggests that "religion is not about God." Rue documents how evolution has shaped human beings in such a way that religion is about influencing the brain "for the sake of personal wholeness and social coherence." His view is similar to the perspective of this book.

Being an agnostic or an atheist does not, however, make one a humanist. I am a humanist because I believe in the inherent worth and dignity of every person, because I believe life is most worth living when we strive to make the world a better place, and because I believe the only possibility for a world in which love, justice, peace, and freedom prevail is through human beings working together to transform the world. *If religion is about affirming the sacred and encountering the holy, I believe as a humanistic religious naturalist that the universe and human life are sacred and living humanly is holy.*

For me the myths, symbols, stories, and doctrines of the traditional Western religions no longer have meaning and power, and I cannot accept the existence of a supernatural realm. But the best values of Western religion continue to make sense to me, and I find those values in a humanistic perspective.

To be religious does not require that one accept the existence of a supernatural being. To be religious is a matter of one's attitude toward all of life. The religious aspect of humanism consists of an appreciation of the dignity and worth of every person; reverence and wonder at the world of nature, at human creativity, and at life itself; a sense of the unity of all things; joy in human community; and a commitment to a cause that transcends the self. More than belief in a deity, I believe these values define what it means to be religious.

Humanistic Religious Naturalism

In addition to being a religious humanist, I am also a religious naturalist, which means that I find religious meaning and values in nature. My naturalistic understanding enriches and deepens my humanist beliefs. I call my belief system *humanistic religious naturalism*. A fully elaborated humanistic religious naturalism is a way of life with both depth and meaning, encompassing a solid theoretical foundation and a great deal of practical wisdom. It is a way to live a meaningful life and a perspective that enables us to understand our place in society and in the universe. In the past, religious humanism has been accused of being dry and sterile and overly rationalistic. Merging religious humanism with religious naturalism overcomes these problems by adding to humanism a language of reverence, a deeper spiritual dimension, and a rich and meaningful story, as we shall see in the chapter entitled "Anchored in Nature."

The Religious Dimension

MY NEIGHBOR who asked me what it means to be a humanist was puzzled that one could be both a humanist and a minister. "I thought humanism was a secular ideology, yet you talk about being a religious humanist. I don't get it. Does that just mean that you're an atheist who goes to church?" I replied that one difference between religious and secular humanism is indeed that religious humanists usually find participation in a religious community to be a meaningful part of their lives. I went on to explain that there are other religious aspects of the lives of religious humanists— aspects that are usually missing from the lives of secular humanists. However, the answer to my neighbor's question really depends on how one defines religion.

There have been many attempts to define religion. Each of these definitions reflects one of three types of religion: *intellectual, affective,* or *practical* religion. Intellectual religion emphasizes beliefs and doctrines; affective religion is understood mainly in terms of feelings and emotions; and practical religion is primarily a matter of ethical action. All three of these qualities are found in all religions, but usually one is dominant.

Religious humanism places a good deal of importance on intelligence in its task of separating truth from falsehood, but it rejects creedal statements. It also regards affect as important in both its search for truth and its ethical decision making. But it is the practical aspect that predominates, because of the high priority religious humanism places on moral living and ethical action. If religion is equated with belief in a supernatural deity, religious humanism cannot be considered religious. But while such a definition of religion is the popular one in the United States, it is not universal. Confucianism, Taoism, Jainism, and some forms of Buddhism, for example, are not theistic. Moreover, numerous definitions of religion do not include reference to a deity.

Protestant theologian Paul Tillich spoke of religion as the dimension of depth in life, and therefore as having to do with one's ultimate concern. For philosopher and theologian Rudolf Otto, religion consists of a profound awareness of a sense of mystery to which one responds with awe and wonder. Mircea Eliade, a scholar of the history of religions, maintained that religion has to do with the acknowledgement of the sacred or the holy, however that might be understood. Unitarian Universalist minister Forrest Church defines religion as "our human response to the dual reality of being alive and having to die."

Others define religion as the search for that which gives meaning and purpose to one's life. Humanist professor Anthony Pinn, drawing on Harvard theologian Gordon Kaufman, defines religion as "that which provides orientation or direction for human life" along with "motivation for living and acting in accordance with this orientation." By this definition, religious humanism is clearly a religion.

As I see it, religion refers to becoming more fully human through living as intensely, as joyfully, and as responsibly as possible, and it includes the affective and the ethical as well as the intellectual dimensions.

John Dewey

The philosopher John Dewey's understanding of religion and the religious, as developed in his 1934 Terry Lectures at Yale and published as *A Common Faith*, is instructive for religious humanists. Dewey distinguishes between the noun *religion* and the adjective *religious*. In his usage, *religion* refers to the institutional religions, which are characterized by specific beliefs and practices that include the idea of the supernatural. Dewey rejects supernaturalism and organized religions, but he maintains that there is a religious quality in everyday experiences. While traditional views separate religion from secular life and put it in a compartment labeled the sacred, Dewey insists that all experiences—aesthetic, political, moral, scientific, and social—are potentially religious. There need be no split between the sacred and the secular. Dewey describes religious faith as "devotion to the ideal" and claims, "Any activity pursued in behalf of an ideal end . . . because of convictions of its general and enduring value is religious in quality." For example, music that is specifically "religious," such as hymns, anthems, chorales, and chants, is not necessarily religious in Dewey's sense unless it truly helps to enlarge one's perspective and to unify the self. However, Dewey would consider any music that accomplishes those things to be religious. Thus, a Beethoven symphony or a Mozart piano concerto can be religious, whereas Handel's *Messiah* or Bach's "Jesu, Joy of Man's Desiring" may not necessarily be. It depends on the effect on the listener or performer.

Dewey further suggests that religions frequently prevent the religious quality of experience from becoming conscious because what might otherwise be experienced as religious is interpreted in the terms of a particular religion. By his understanding, many people who have nothing to do with religion are unaware that they have attitudes that are genuinely religious. Dewey's approach liberates the religious quality of experience from its imprisonment within organized religion, where it is misunderstood or converted into a calcified doctrine. Dewey would not consider religious humanism a *religion* but he would call it *religious* because it is devoted to the ideals of human worth and dignity, freedom, justice, and peace. Thus Dewey would draw no distinction between secular and religious humanism.

The religious, then, is a quality of experience rather than a particular institutional embodiment or a set of beliefs. Dewey insists that religious experience does not include assenting to any facts; that is the role of science. Rather, *religious experience* refers to the attitude one may take toward just about anything. It is the effect that an experience produces that can make it religious:

> The way in which the experience operated, its function, determines its religious value. If the reorientation actually occurs, it, and the sense of security and stability accompanying it, are forces on their own account. It takes place in different persons in a multitude of ways. It is sometimes brought about by devotion to a cause; sometimes by a passage of poetry that opens a new perspective; sometimes as was the case with Spinoza—deemed an atheist in his day— through philosophical reflection.

Those experiences that enhance one's life, that result in a greater unification within the self and of the self with the world, that are profoundly moral in nature, that are transforming, or that lead to a better adjustment to the conditions of life—those experiences are religious.

By adjustment to life, Dewey does not mean stoic resignation but rather a profound acceptance of one's self, of the universe, and of one's place in the universe. As a social activist committed to transforming an unjust society, Dewey is not counseling complacency but instead a unification of the various aspects of the self into a harmonious whole. Adjustment to life, for Dewey, involves a reorientation through which the individual becomes more unified, productive, and fulfilled. For me, activities on behalf of social justice have been religious in Dewey's sense. So have preparing and writing sermons, conversing with friends and others about their significant life experiences, reading great literature, and experiencing the beauty and wonder of nature.

Most importantly, Dewey believes that religious experience includes moral conviction and action:

But belief or faith has also a moral and practical import. . . . Conviction in the moral sense signifies being conquered, vanquished, in our active nature by an ideal end; it signifies acknowledgement of its rightful claim over our desires and purposes. Such acknowledgement is practical, not primarily intellectual.

Religious faith then involves being devoted to a significant cause, an ideal goal, something larger than one's own ego that captures the self and to which we give our complete allegiance.

Clearly, religious humanism is not a *religion* in Dewey's sense, because it has no institutional embodiment, rejects supernaturalism, and does not have an official creed or set of rituals. It is *religious* in Dewey's sense in that it considers all experience in every sphere of life as potentially of a religious quality, is grounded in attitudes that are life enhancing and devoted to ideal ends, and has deeply felt moral convictions that lead to unification of the self and of the self with the world.

Another way of describing the religious dimension is to identify certain qualities, attitudes, or characteristics of human experience that have traditionally been thought of as religious. These include mystery, a sense of oneness with all things, values, a sense of meaning, community, and gratitude. Secular humanism does not include all of these characteristics, and thus this understanding of what is religious helps to distinguish religious from secular humanism.

Mystery

Since the beginning of recorded history, part of the religious impulse in humankind has been to be open to the mystery that lies in and around us and to respond to that mystery with feelings of reverence and astonishment. Ancient people felt awe and wonder as they saw lightning and heard thunder or felt a strong wind. Even though we understand the workings of nature far better than the ancients did, many of us still experience the world as marvelous. Albert Einstein writes in "What I Believe,"

The most beautiful thing we can experience is the mysterious. It is the source of all true art and science. He to whom this emotion is a stranger, who can no longer pause to wonder and stand rapt in awe, is as good as dead. . . . To know that what is impenetrable to us really exists, manifesting itself as the highest wisdom and the most radiant beauty which our dull faculties can comprehend only in their most primitive forms—this knowledge, this feeling, is at the center of true religiousness. In this sense, and in this sense only, I belong to the ranks of the devoutly religious men.

Although I know more than the ancients did about the universe, the process of reproduction, and the nature of the human body, I am still filled with awe when I gaze at the night sky or at the infant grandchild I hold in my arms, or when I ponder the intricate biology of the human body or the incredible structure of the human brain. I often go outside on a clear night and gaze at the sky glittering with the lights of thousands of stars, most of them larger than our sun. As I ponder the unimaginable vastness of what I am seeing and the incredible distances between the stars, I am overcome with awe and amazement and with a sense of how tiny the earth is and how infinitesimally small I am. I am cleansed of pride and arrogance and filled with a sweet sense of humility.

I find that the more I learn about the world from modern science, the more I am in awe. That the star Arcturus, which I can see in the night sky, is 216 trillion miles away absolutely boggles my mind. That other stars I can see with the naked eye are as far away as ten thousand light years leaves me speechless. That there are trillions of cells in my body and that there is enough DNA in those cells to reach to the sun and back a dozen times if stretched out—these facts fill me with wonder and astonishment.

Knowledge and understanding do not decrease wonder and the sense of the mystery in which we live; in fact, they often increase these religious sensitivities. Two books by scientists that illustrate this point are *The Sacred Depths of Nature* by microbiologist Ursula Goodenough and *Skeptics and True Believers* by physicist Chet Raymo. Raymo writes that we can think of "all scientific knowledge that we have of this world, or will ever have ... as an island in the sea of mystery."

Nor does having a skeptical mind, a characteristic of most secular and religious humanists, negate the ability to experience wonder. As W. MacNeile Dixon writes, "If there be a skeptical star I was born under it, yet I have lived all my days in complete astonishment." Even though science can take what we experience as deeply moving and, by turning its cold objective eye on it, treat it as impersonal and meaningless, the opposite can happen too. Einstein noted that science increases wonder by allowing us to catch a glimpse of a marvelous, cosmic order we could not have imagined without it.

To be struck with a sense of mystery and reverence at the natural world or at human creations is an experience that is religious in nature, and one that is common to many who identify as religious humanists.

Oneness with All That Is

The word *religion* comes from the root word, *religio*, meaning to bind together. To be religious is to have a sense that all persons and all of life are bound together. We find this sense of oneness in the experience of the great mystics who felt themselves to be at one with God or with the whole of existence. The unity of the Brahman-Atman relationship within Hinduism and the sense of Nirvana in Buddhism are examples of mystical union. Many of us, myself included, who will never attain total mystical vision have experienced something of that feeling—some fleeting moments when we have a sense of being a part of everything and everyone. Casey, the former preacher in John Steinbeck's *The Grapes of Wrath*, gives voice to this feeling as he lies on his back in the open hills, looking up at the stars at night and the sun in the morning: "There was the hills, an' there was me, an' we wasn't separate no more. We was one thing. An' that one thing was holy."

The mystical experience does not depend on the existence of a supernatural realm but can be understood within a purely naturalistic framework. Dewey writes that far from denying the existence of mystical experiences, "there is every reason to suppose that, in some degree of intensity, they occur so frequently that they may be regarded as normal manifestations that take place at certain rhythmic points in the movement of experience."

Humanistic psychologist Abraham Maslow used the term "peak experiences" to describe the feeling of losing a sense of ego, time, and space, experiencing a heightened consciousness and the sensation of being at one with all things. For Maslow, peak experiences are natural, not supernatural, experiences.

Many religious humanists have a deep and abiding sense of the unity of all things. This often takes the form of a sense of oneness with the natural world, of being part of the woods, the sky, and the land. Many of us also feel a sense of unity with other people. I like to think of myself as a single cell in a body of seven billion cells. I exult in being an individual, but I also glory in feeling a part of humankind. As a Unitarian Universalist, I think of the contemporary meaning of *Unitarian* as referring to the fundamental unity of all people and all things. A deep sense of the unity of all life becomes a basis for a commitment to both environmental preservation and human betterment.

Values

Religious humanism draws on the Hebrew and Christian traditions, with their insistence that religion and ethics go together. The great Hebrew prophets taught that Yahweh God requires justice, mercy, and kindness, and that religion consists not of ritual and ceremony but of doing good toward one's neighbor. Speaking for Yahweh, the prophet Amos cried out against religious rites and demanded justice instead:

> I hate, I despise your feasts, and I take no delight in your
> solemn assemblies. Even though you offer me your burnt

offerings and cereal offerings, I will not accept them. . . . But let justice roll down like waters and righteousness like an ever-flowing stream.

Jesus continued that tradition by teaching that the commandment second in importance only to love of God is to love one's neighbor as oneself. He defined one's neighbor as anyone in need, even an enemy, as illustrated in the parable of the Good Samaritan. By caring for the injured traveler, the Samaritan engages in a religious act.

Since the foundational conviction of religious humanism is a belief in the dignity and value of every person, it draws no boundaries or limitations as to who is a proper object of love and compassion. Neither race, nor nationality, nor religious or philosophical persuasion, nor gender, nor sexual orientation should make any difference when it comes to love and concern for others. Religious humanism teaches and practices ethical universalism, the understanding that love, equality, and justice must be extended to all persons without distinction. Religious humanists should be deeply concerned with human rights throughout the world, with democratic values and human freedom, with economic justice and equality for all persons. Humanistic ethics have both a social and an individual dimension.

As the minister emeritus of a largely humanistic congregation, I have seen humanists caring for people experiencing crises; rallying for equal rights for women; working in soup kitchens feeding the homeless; lobbying legislators for equal rights for bisexual, gay, lesbian, and transgender people; and giving themselves in many other ways to promote the things they believe in. They believe in living their humanistic values and working to extend them to others. For religious humanists, ethical principles constitute an important part of what it means to be religious.

Meaning and Purpose

It has always been the function of religion to provide a reason for living. According to the famous formulation of John Calvin, the

Christian lives in order "to glorify God and enjoy Him forever." Other theologians have said that we live in order to do God's will and play a role in God's divine plan. Abraham Maslow found that the people he described as "self-actualizing," people who were more fully functioning, creative, and fulfilled, were devoted to some cause or ideal outside themselves. Theoretically, that cause may be material acquisition or fame or power. But for the cause to be truly fulfilling and lasting, it must be something that contributes to human well-being. The religious humanist will find meaning and purpose in something that is not grounded in self-interest, a cause that enriches life and the world. That cause may be working to provide low-cost housing, advocating for racial justice, serving on a church caring committee, creating works of beauty, tutoring children, or any one of a number of other things.

Community

The conviction that life is lived best with others who share one's values is an essential quality of religious life. Since religious humanists believe that we have no supernatural presence among us, human community becomes all the more important. While there are other forms of human community that are meaningful, religious community offers the possibility of realizing a greater depth and meaning than others. I believe that to be fully human, we must be in true community with others. As an African axiom puts it, "I am because we are."

We need one another to help diminish our sorrows and to increase our joys. It is meaningful to celebrate life's passages with others who share our values. Moreover, since we live in a culture in which humanists are a small minority, knowing others who share our convictions is supportive and reinforcing.

Religious humanists find meaning and value in celebrating rites of passage: birth, coming of age, marriage, and death. Birth celebrations include naming and recognition ceremonies; coming of age ceremonies celebrate the end of training in humanistic values and ethics. Marriage and death rites are personalized as opposed to passages read from a traditional ceremony. Like most Unitarian Universalist ministers, I do not use the same "boiler-plate" texts for memorial services. In each service, I speak about the life of the deceased and select readings that fit the unique individual whose life is being celebrated. Humanist religious communities may give humanistic interpretations to traditional holidays such as Christmas and Easter. For me as a Unitarian Universalist minister, Christmas is a time to celebrate new life and the possibility of "divine" ideals, such as love and justice, becoming incarnate in everyone, not just in one person. Easter becomes a celebration of the possibility of personal renewal and the beauty and joys of nature. Humanists may also celebrate days that have universal human meaning—such as Earth Day, May Day, which celebrates human solidarity in numerous countries, and United Nations Day, which symbolizes the unity and cooperation of all the world's people.

Additionally, a humanistic religious community may find ways to celebrate its roots in biological and cosmic evolution and its history in the expansion of human freedoms. One church I know celebrates the anniversary of the Emancipation Proclamation annually. A number of churches, both theistic and nontheistic, are now celebrating an annual "evolution day" or "Darwin Day" near Darwin's birthday in early February, a day that celebrates the story of how we and the earth came to be. A humanistic community will honor those people who have contributed much to religious humanism and to a particular community, and it will find symbols that represent its values and that speak to its heart.

Gratitude

On my desk sits a framed card that says, "Just to be is a blessing. Just to live is holy," a saying attributed to the Jewish mystic and social activist Abraham Joshua Heschel. It is a reminder to me of the element of grace in my life—that my life itself is a gift over which

I had no control but for which I am exceedingly grateful, and that much that has happened to me personally and professionally has been a gift as well. In every service of worship I conduct, I remind worshippers, myself included, that we have much for which to be thankful. Something of this awareness of grace and gratitude is part of the religious dimension of the kind of religious humanism I am describing. An attitude of gratitude is life-transforming.

These characteristics, then, describe six kinds of experiences that are religious, and by this understanding many humanists would qualify as religious. This approach to religion is somewhat different from that of John Dewey, but there is some overlapping of the two approaches; they are not mutually exclusive. I think of this approach as supplementing Dewey's perspective. No discussion of religion would be complete, however, if we did not add that like everything else in life, to be religious is to be engaged in a process—a joyous lifelong process of growing and deepening.

A vital and viable religious faith must have four components: a cosmology, the story of who we are and why we are here; a spiritual dimension, the conviction of a deeper meaning to life than everyday existence; an ethic, the rationale for living responsibly and with compassion; and public celebrations of shared values and of life's passages.

For the religious humanist, the story of who we are is the scientific story of cosmic and biological evolution, and it inspires awe and reverence. The spiritual dimension includes responding to the mystery of life with both gratitude and wonder and finding meaning and joy in living and in justice-seeking. Living ethically follows from our basic principles and is central to our faith, and public expressions of our faith enrich our lives and strengthen our commitments.

A Short History

IN DIFFERENT FORMS and with various designations, humanism has been around in its secular form since at least the time of Confucius—around 500 BCE. Most of that time it has been thought of as a philosophy, but within the last hundred years, it has blossomed as an explicitly religious perspective. Its emergence and development form an interesting story.

In the West, the ancient Greeks were the first to hold views that can be called humanistic. Anaxagoras, Protagoras, and Democritus expressed skepticism about the gods of the Greek pantheon, and Protagoras famously suggested that "man is the measure of all things." Nevertheless, Greek thought was dominated by Socrates and Plato, who affirmed an ideal supernatural realm.

Humanism next appeared in the West during the Renaissance, exemplified by Erasmus. Renaissance humanism emphasized this world rather than the next, valued reason, and encouraged critical study of ancient texts. It held that humans are not morally depraved, as traditional Christianity maintained, but rather beings of ethical and intellectual worth. Renaissance humanism was theistic, however, and therefore quite removed from today's humanism.

The Protestant Reformation played a key role in the eventual birth of religious humanism. The basis of the Reformation was what Luther called the "priesthood of all believers." By that he

meant that people do not need ordained priests serving as media-
tors between individuals and God, as the Catholic church taught;
he believed that each person has direct access to the divine. The
implication of this teaching is that each person is responsible for
his or her own religious life. In this understanding, religious faith
is a personal and individual matter. It would take centuries for the
full implications of this radical idea to be felt, but the seeds were
sown in the sixteenth century.

However, it was the philosophers and theologians of the eight-
eenth and nineteenth centuries who laid the major foundation of
twentieth-century religious humanism. One impetus came from
the philosopher Immanuel Kant, who refuted the traditional arguments for the existence of God, although he found other
grounds—"the starry sky above and the moral law within"—to
believe in the deity. The skeptical thought of David Hume and the
empiricism of John Locke helped to create the modern skeptical
and empirical worldview. That skepticism was further fueled by
Ludwig Feuerbach, whose book *The Essence of Christianity* suggests that God is a human invention, a projection on the cosmos
of the best attributes and highest values human beings can imagine. Nietzsche also contributed to the background of modern humanism with his proclamation of the death of God and his view
that Judaism and Christianity are "slave religions" because of their
insistence on uncritical submission to absolute authority.

The great German theologian Friedrich Schleiermacher responded to the Kantian critique by maintaining that religion is
not a matter of beliefs but rather is grounded in a preconscious
experience he called "the feeling of absolute dependence." Thus
Schleiermacher expanded Luther's principle of the priesthood of
all believers by understanding religion as an internal experience
for each individual. That helped to lay the foundation for religious
humanism by freeing religion from a system of doctrines. From
Schleiermacher it was but a short step to John Dewey's understanding of "the religious" as a particular quality of experience
rather than a set of beliefs.

The historical, critical, and textual study of the Bible known as biblical criticism also played an important role in the birth of religious humanism. Scholars determined that the gospels were written long after Jesus' death and that the events, stories, and especially the miracles reported in them were to a large extent the product of the imaginative prescientific minds of his early followers. In studying the culture of the time, they also found that the myth of the dying and rising god was widespread in other religious cults of the first century. In this and other ways, the historical critical study of the Bible cast doubt on the authenticity of the Christian message.

However, modern science and the scientific-empirical method are the most important catalysts in the development of modern humanism. Copernicus's discovery that the sun, not the earth, was the center of the solar system led to doubt about the truth of the Bible, with its description of the earth and humankind as the center of the universe. But it was Darwin's theory of natural selection that led many away from such central Christian beliefs as the biblical creation story and the understanding of human beings as the special creation of God. Accepting natural selection requires one to recognize that the earth is far older than the biblical creation story implies. And Darwinian evolution sees humans simply as part of the natural world. This understanding casts grave doubt on the Greek idea, adopted by much of Christendom, that human beings consist of a transient physical body inhabited by a noncorporeal, eternal soul. If the human mind and human consciousness are the products of evolution—if we are entirely natural beings rather than part natural and part supernatural—then the whole Christian edifice of immortality, divine creation, and human beings made in the image of God is called into question.

A number of Unitarians welcomed the insights of *The Origin of Species*, as did those "fellow travelers" Ralph Waldo Emerson and Henry David Thoreau. In 1874 Minot Savage, minister of the Church of the Messiah in New York City, published a collection of sermons entitled *The Faith of Evolution*, which became a best seller in 1876 under the title *The Religion of Evolution*. Critical of those liberal religionists who rejected Darwin's findings, Savage lists many scientific breakthroughs originally opposed by the church but now accepted as fact and argues that evolution is just such a breakthrough that should be embraced. Savage believed that religion needed to adapt to the new discoveries of science in order to remain a vital force in human affairs.

Quite apart from the conflict over evolution, the ideas of Ralph Waldo Emerson and the Transcendentalists were instrumental in the rise of religious humanism. Emerson's critique of the authoritarianism of the church and the Bible, along with the Transcendentalists' vision of the divinity of humanity, the importance of free inquiry, and personal religious experience, helped to pave the way for humanism. So also did Emerson's view of the divine as immanent in the world rather than a separate transcendent being and Theodore Parker's view that the Christian faith would still be valid even if Jesus had never lived. Parker affirmed a "permanent" religious core independent of the "transient" Christian tradition, and in so doing helped to lay the foundation of a future religious humanism.

Not all of these cultural and religious innovations were explicitly humanistic. But they cultivated the religious and philosophical soil out of which the liberal religious humanism of the twentieth century could grow.

Freethinkers in America

Late eighteenth-century America produced two outspoken and famous critics of religion, Thomas Paine and Ethan Allen. In *The Age of Reason*, Paine denounces all revealed religions and insists that Christianity, like all religions, is a human invention rather than a revelation of God. Nevertheless, Paine also affirms his belief in "the God of nature—a God who is served by helping others in this life rather than obeisance to churches that promise eternal life." Allen's *Reason the Only Oracle of Man* also castigates

Christianity, particularly the hellfire-and-damnation brand of Calvinism with which he was most familiar, and criticizes "the tyranny of Priests" who try to "invalidate the law of nature and reason in order to establish systems incompatible therewith." Although not known as humanists, a number of nineteenth-century women and men proclaimed what amounted to a nontheistic humanism, and their work, while vilified by many in the larger culture, helped lay the groundwork for religious humanism. Among them were several remarkable women who regarded religion as one of the major forces keeping women in submission to men. Frances Wright was the first woman to speak publicly to men and women in lecture halls in this country, the first to advocate women's equality publicly, and the first to publicly denounce religion and its clergy. Finding in religion the source of conflict, violence, and war, she advocated turning "churches into halls of science and . . . teachers of faith [into] expounders of nature." Defining faith as "a belief in, and homage rendered to, existences unseen and causes unknown," she insisted on speaking only about what she *knew* and recommended that others do the same.

One of the most extraordinary of these women was Polish-born Ernestine L. Rose. An eloquent and charismatic speaker, she unapologetically used the term *atheist* to characterize her religious perspective, defining atheism as "a disbelief in God, because finding no demonstration of his existence, man's reason will not allow him to believe, nor his conviction to play the hypocrite, and profess what he does not believe." She believed that humankind had created God in its own image, not vice versa, and her lecture entitled "A Defense of Atheism" concludes with these words, which could also be taken as a statement of humanism:

> In conclusion, the Atheist says to the honest conscientious believer, Though I cannot believe in your God whom you have failed to demonstrate, I believe in man; if I have no faith in your religion, I have faith, unbounded, unshaken faith in the principles of right, of justice, and humanity. . . . Whatever good you would do out of fear of punishment, or hope of re-

ward hereafter, the Atheist would do simply because it is good; and being so, he would receive the far surer and more certain reward, springing from well-doing, which would constitute his pleasure, and promote his happiness.

Much better known to us today is Elizabeth Cady Stanton, who held the church responsible for much of the subjugation of women, which she saw as beginning with the biblical account in which Eve is blamed for the entrance of sin into the world. Far from seeing Eve's act as the fall of humankind, as Christian theology taught, Stanton maintains in "The Polling Booth" that the act of eating the apple was the unlocking to the human family of all the realms of knowledge and thought:

> Yes, when Eve took her destiny in her own hand and set minds spinning down through all the spheres of time, she declared humanity omnipotent, and today thinking people are rapt in wonder and admiration at the inventions and discoveries of science, the grandeur of man's conceptions, and the magnitude of his works.

An advocate for the religion of humanity, Stanton believed that "what we call God is the infinite ideal of humanity." This "new religion will teach the dignity of human nature and its infinite possibilities for development . . . will inspire its worshippers with self-respect, with noble aspirations to attain diviner heights from day to day than they yet have reached. . . . Its creed will be Justice, Liberty, Equality for all the children of the earth." Although she did not use the term *religious humanism*, her "religion of humanity" seems to be just that; its essence was an affirmation of human dignity, freedom from fear and superstition, and freedom of belief.

America's greatest poet, Walt Whitman, also belongs to this tradition. In *Leaves of Grass*, he writes of the priesthood of all people and the divinity of all men and women. The guardians of orthodox religion objected to his celebration of the human to the exclusion of deity.

No discussion of freethinking in the nineteenth century can

omit "the Great Agnostic," Robert G. Ingersoll, the undisputed preeminent orator of his era. In the 1880s and 1890s especially, Ingersoll traveled and lectured widely in small towns and large cities. As an agnostic, he said that he did not know whether or not God exists, but that if he did, he could not understand why God would allow so much pain and suffering and injustice and oppression. He observed that "each nation has created a god, and the god has always resembled his creators. He hated and loved what they hated and loved, and he was invariably on the side of those in power." Yet Ingersoll could also state that "the universe is all the God there is."

The only religion Ingersoll could recommend was what he called "the religion of humanity." Today we call it humanism. Calling all other religion superstition, he maintained that the religion of humanity was the only religion that made sense. This was to be a religion in which human beings were to be treated with dignity and respect, in which people were responsible for themselves and one another:

> If the naked are clothed, man will clothe them; if the hungry are fed, man must feed them. I prefer to rely on human endeavor, upon human intelligence, upon the heart and brain of man. There is no evidence that God ever interfered in the affairs of man. The hand of earth is stretched uselessly towards heaven. From the clouds there comes no help. In vain the shipwrecked cry to God. In vain the imprisoned ask for liberty and light—the world moves on, and the heavens are deaf, dumb, and blind. The frost freezes, the fire burns, slander smites, the wrong triumphs, the good suffer, and prayer dies upon the lips of faith.

By the last half of the nineteenth century, the United States was prepared for the emergence of religious humanism as a viable movement.

The Free Religious Association

In 1865 Henry Whitney Bellows, the prominent minister of All Souls Unitarian Church in New York City, concerned with the fragmentation of the young Unitarian movement, organized the National Conference of Unitarian Churches. The National Conference adopted a statement affirming allegiance to "Our Lord Jesus Christ," to which the liberal wing of the Unitarian movement objected. When the National Conference refused to drop the statement, the liberals formed the Free Religious Association (FRA), which repudiated the idea of a creedal statement of any kind. The FRA was composed of ministers and others who had been influenced by Emerson and Parker and who believed that religious truth was to be found in Hinduism, Buddhism, and Islam as well as in Judaism and Christianity. In fact, Emerson was the first to sign the document establishing the Free Religious Association. In 1894 the American Unitarian Association (AUA) finally dropped the objectionable creedal statement, and once again no doctrinal test was required to be a member or a minister in the Association. That move was important because it would make it possible for the religious humanists who emerged a generation later to remain within the AUA.

One of the leading voices of the FRA, Francis Ellingwood Abbot, castigated the statement affirming allegiance to Christ, saying it proved "that even the most liberal church could not come to terms with 'the modern spirit.'" Abbot's book *Scientific Theism* welcomes biological evolution and anticipates modern process philosophy with an understanding of the universe as an evolving organism and God as a force of "infinite intelligibility" within the universe rather than a supernatural being. By proclaiming "the new Gospel of religion and science, the Gospel of faith in man," Abbot comes very close to religious humanism.

Commitment to "the adaptation of religious ideas to modern culture" was central to the FRA, including especially "the rise of science in a new form—evolutionary naturalism." Darwin himself subscribed to the FRA newsletter, and in response to an article in it dealing with evolution and religion, he wrote that he agreed with most of what was written.

The members of the FRA were neither Christian Unitarians nor religious humanists; they were theists of one kind or another. But their importance for Unitarian religious humanism is twofold: They insisted that Unitarianism should not be shackled by a creed, and they were open to and accepting of the discoveries of modern science. So when humanism arose in Unitarianism, the humanists could not be forced out on the grounds that they did not subscribe to a creedal formulation.

Modernism and Naturalism

In the early twentieth century, Christian theologians responded to Darwin, modern science, and biblical criticism with what was called modernism in religion. Religious modernism accepted evolution but held that the hand of God guided the evolutionary process. It accepted biblical criticism as well but still revered the Bible as a source of inspiration and insight.

Shailer Matthews and D. C. MacIntosh were modernism's leading theologians. Matthews stressed the importance of science and democracy but maintained that these were not sufficient to change the world without love of God and neighbor. MacIntosh sought to base Christian theology in empirical human experience as the source of our knowledge of God.

Harry Emerson Fosdick, a popular pulpit and radio preacher, a writer, and minister of the Riverside Church in New York City, was the best known Christian modernist. Fosdick, who held the essence of Christianity to be "reverence for personality," drew on the insights of psychology in emphasizing a gospel of personal wholeness and religious maturity. Rejecting the idea that Christianity consisted of accepting orthodox doctrines, Fosdick regarded Jesus not as the divine second person of the Trinity but as the best human representation of the divine and the greatest teacher of the value of persons.

Meanwhile, at the Divinity School of the University of Chicago, several prominent theologians were developing a "school" of religious naturalism. Although theistic, these theologians rejected supernaturalism, and so their conception of deity was of a god immanent in the natural universe. Among them were Edward Scribner Ames, Bernard Meland, and Henry Nelson Wieman. For Wieman—who grounded his theology in empiricism, ruling out metaphysical speculation—the term *God* referred to the process of what he called "creative interchange," by which he meant a power operating in the world to increase value and other forms of human good.

Two other thinkers, Bertrand Russell and Harvard philosopher George Santayana, deserve mention for their influence on the worldview that gave rise to religious humanism. Russell's 1903 essay, "A Free Man's Worship," articulates both his atheistic naturalism and his deep faith in human possibilities. In *Reason in Religion*, published in 1905, Santayana rejects a literal view of religion and suggests that religion is valuable primarily as poetry and moral insight.

African American Humanism

Anthony Pinn notes that while most of American humanism arose from the emphasis on reason and scientific empiricism stemming from the Enlightenment, African American humanism came from the inability to reconcile the experience of oppression with belief in a just and powerful God. African American humanism was a repudiation of Christianity, which slaves and others identified with the persecution of African Americans. In 1839 Bishop Daniel Payne expressed his concern that the Christian church was losing the slaves because "they hear their masters professing Christianity; they see these masters preaching the gospel; they hear these masters praying in their families, and they know that oppression and slavery are inconsistent with the Christian religion; therefore they scoff at religion itself—mock their masters, and distrust both the goodness and justice of God." Pinn mentions Frederick Douglass, Zora Neale Hurston, W. E. B. DuBois, and A. Philip Randolph as examples of African American humanists, and suggests the Harlem Renaissance as the period in which African American humanism reached its zenith.

Social conditions led other African Americans to embrace humanist convictions. Civil rights leader James Forman writes that he became a humanist because he felt that belief in God and the hereafter hampered the commitment of African Americans to change their lives in the here and now. Humanism, on the other hand, meant for him a commitment to change present conditions for the better. Anthony Pinn himself became a humanist because he could not accept the idea of a just and merciful God who permitted suffering and oppression; nor could he view the suffering of African Americans as in any way redemptive, as the black church and much of Christian theology taught. "After taking a deep breath," he writes, "I spoke a new word: God does not exist."

The earliest African American Unitarian minister who identified as a humanist was Lewis McGee, the son of an African Methodist Episcopal minister who was also a former slave. In 1927 McGee, in his early thirties, discovered Curtis Reese's book *Humanist Sermons* and realized that it described his religious perspective. Unable to get a Unitarian pulpit, McGee worked as a social worker, continued to pastor AME congregations, and served on the board of the American Humanist Association. After acting as a chaplain in the Second World War (he had also served in that capacity in the first war), he returned to Chicago and in 1947 founded the Free Religious Fellowship, an African American congregation on Chicago's South Side. He later served several churches in California until his retirement. His humanism can be seen in such sermons as "Have Faith in Man" and "We Choose Our Destiny."

While agreeing that the origin of black humanism stems from the inadequacy of Christianity, Unitarian Universalist professor William R. Jones regards liberation as its goal, and he maintains that "the oppressed are oppressed, in fundamental part, because of the beliefs they hold. They . . . accept a belief system that stifles their motivation to attack the institutions and groups that oppress them." That belief system results in humility, submission, and obedience, but includes the promise of heaven for those who suffer in this life. The task then becomes one of freeing "the mind of the oppressed from the enslaving ideas and submissive attitudes that sabotage any movement towards authentic freedom." Thus, for Jones, African American humanism is not only an intellectual position; it is also an activist liberation theology.

The founder and leader of a group called African Americans for Humanism is Norm Allen Jr., who authored "An African American Humanist Declaration." The Declaration acknowledges the origin of black humanism in slavery and racism and articulates general humanist ethical principles, plus six principles specifically addressed to the African American community. It declares opposition to racism in all its forms and suggests that humanism can be a more inclusive vehicle for uniting the African American community than the Christian churches have been.

Early Unitarian Humanism

With the intellectual background of an empirical and naturalistic worldview described earlier, it is not surprising that a creedless religion would soon spawn religious humanism. The earliest Unitarians who identified themselves as humanists were John Dietrich, often called the father of religious humanism, and Curtis Reese. Dietrich had been raised in the Reformed tradition and was a minister in that tradition for several years. However, even in seminary he had begun to question some of the orthodox Christian doctrines. At the age of thirty-three he resigned his Reformed Church pastorate rather than subject his congregation and himself to the embarrassment of a heresy trial. A Unitarian colleague suggested he become a Unitarian, which he did, and in September 1911 he became minister of the Unitarian church in Spokane, Washington. He soon began referring to his religion as humanism. In 1916 he was invited to the pulpit of the First Unitarian Society of Minneapolis, where he developed further his humanistic religious views.

Curtis Reese had been brought up a Southern Baptist in North Carolina, but like Dietrich, he began to have questions about his faith while in seminary. After seminary he served as a Baptist pastor for a while, but realized that he was too liberal to continue. He became a Unitarian in 1913 at age twenty-six and served Unitarian churches in the Midwest for several years. In 1919 he became the secretary of the Western Unitarian Conference. Wherever he served, Reese was active in social concerns. In 1930 he became dean of the Abraham Lincoln Center in Chicago, a center for social activism and adult education. He stayed in that position until 1957, when his health forced him to retire.

At first Reese referred to his humanism as a "religion of democracy." In a 1916 sermon he contrasts his democratic religion with autocratic religion:

> The theocratic view of the world order is autocratic. The humanistic view is democratic. In the theocratic order God is the autocrat; and under him are various minor autocrats, called divinities, angels, spirits, fairies, demons, and the like. In the democratic order the people are the rulers of their own affairs, and above them are no autocrats, supreme or minor, whose favor they must curry.

In a significant and controversial address to the Harvard Divinity School in 1920, Reese held that lack of a creed and insistence on individual freedom of belief was the essence of liberal religion. He went on to affirm a naturalistic religion, proclaiming that the purpose of religion is not to glorify God but to promote the development of personality through devotion to worthwhile causes and to advance human welfare here and now.

Shortly thereafter, Dietrich published an article in the *Christian Register*, the Unitarian magazine. The article refers to two kinds of religion. One, he suggests, thrives on human weakness and failure and is built on threats of punishment. It teaches that human beings must rely on a supernatural power who is the source of all our blessings and who promises us a better life in the hereafter. The second kind of religion has faith in people and "looks for no help or consolation from without." Rather than teaching humans to rely on God, "whence no help comes," it promotes "a firm and confident reliance upon themselves, in whom lie the possibilities of all things." Dietrich said that people cannot expect to go to a better world beyond this life but should instead create a better world in the here and now. He also maintained that the world would be radically different and considerably better if the churches taught and preached this second type of religion instead of the first.

Rejecting supernaturalism, Dietrich was a naturalist. He believed that what we call mind or spirit or soul is simply the most complex functioning of matter. He believed that the scientific method is the most reliable way to separate truth from falsehood. He held that the Bible, as the work of men, is flawed but contains some helpful insights, along with a great deal of unhelpful as well as contradictory material. He thought there ought to be a "Bible of Man" that would include the best of the sacred texts of all religions.

Dietrich believed that the concept of God began with the fear of primitive people in the face of natural forces, and that it went through various stages—animism, polytheism, henotheism, and finally monotheism. Just as the idea of God evolved, so also did religion. Dietrich felt that humanistic religion should supplant Christianity as the next stage in religion's evolution. He maintained that it was humans who created God, not vice versa, and that moral principles and laws were not handed down by God but rather arose through human interactions. Noting that Christians gave God credit for good times but did not blame him for bad times, Dietrich could not understand why God should be held responsible for the one and not the other. Nor could he understand why God supposedly gave his blessings to people who did not deserve them. He finally concluded, "No, my friends, we are not at the mercy either of a just or unjust God; we are in an indifferent universe to which we must accommodate ourselves."

For Dietrich, the individual person was central. He maintained that modern industrial society, by demanding conformity and standardization, was crushing individuality and leading to mediocrity. A strong social critic, he believed that since the individual is shaped by society, it is important for humanists to work to change society. "Humanism concerns itself, not so much with the petty wrong doing of the individual," he said, "as with the miserable social environment which has made the individual what he is." Human beings are born good, he held, but need education and a healthy society in order to bring out their full potential.

As a philosophical naturalist, Dietrich believed that life ended with death, and he insisted that it was not necessary to live forever for life to be worthwhile. He did, however, emphasize that people live on in the form of their influence. Noting that Milton and many others had more influence after death than in their lifetimes, he observed that the dead "speak to us from the houses of learning, from the pulpits of churches, from the books of the philosophers, from the paintings of the masters, from the stones of the sculptors, from the songs of the musicians."

Dietrich thought that the church has at least three roles to play in humanistic religion. One role is to teach humanistic views centering on the dignity of each person and the unity of all people. Another is to serve the larger community and work to effect social change. Churches, he felt, should be open seven days a week, encouraging the free flow of ideas through study groups, classes, and meetings discussing social issues. A third role of the church is to provide a setting for worship; from a humanistic perspective this means directing one's mind and emotions toward those qualities that enhance human life. The important thing in worship is to be inspired to make the noblest things in life a part of ourselves.

During this same period—the late teens and early twenties —Roy Wood Sellars, a Unitarian layman and professor of philosophy at the University of Michigan, was also proclaiming religious humanism. His 1918 book, *The Next Step in Religion*, argues that people must give up believing in the supernatural, God, immortality, and absolute truth, and instead embrace a this-worldly, humanistic faith. He did not want to abolish the church, however, which he saw as a center for adult education and social action.

An interview with Sellars by his minister was published in the *Christian Register* and led to responses both pro and con. A number of those responding approved, saying that what Sellars said corresponded to what they had thought for a long time. Others were shocked, offended that a Unitarian publication would print such heretical ideas.

The Theist-Humanist Controversy

In 1921 the controversy between the new humanist views and the older theism took on larger proportions. Curtis Reese invited John Dietrich to speak at a large liberal church in Chicago. In his sermon, Dietrich said that religion must be brought into harmony with modern thought, and that meant that it must give up belief in a supernatural deity and emphasize human powers to achieve happiness and social change.

George Dodson, professor of philosophy at Washington University in St. Louis and a Unitarian layman, strongly expressed his objection, saying that such ideas should not be permitted in a Unitarian pulpit. He went on to write an article for the *Christian Register* attacking religious humanism and insisting that Unitarianism should stand not only for freedom but also for what he called a common faith in God. He insisted that this was not a creedal statement but simply a description of what Unitarians believe. Moreover, he added, if some Unitarian ministers were preaching atheism while others were preaching faith in God, the movement would be torn apart.

Later that same year, the Unitarian National Conference was meeting in Detroit, and Dietrich had been invited to be one of the main speakers. Pressure was put on the general secretary to replace him, but instead the militant theist, William Sullivan, minister of All Souls Church in New York City and a former Roman Catholic priest, was chosen to speak as well. Sullivan had come to Dodson's defense with an article in the *Christian Register* affirming theism and strongly repudiating humanism. Reese had answered that article with a letter affirming the need for religion to enter the modern age. He issued a ringing call to resist any kind of creedal requirements, which he said would lead to heresy trials. Reese concluded his letter by saying that "theism is philosophically possible, but not religiously necessary."

Dodson answered this with a letter arguing that it should be possible to affirm religious freedom while at the same time acknowledging common beliefs. He maintained that the majority of Unitarians accept Jesus' teaching that we are the children of God. He described Unitarianism as the religion of the Twenty-third Psalm, the Lord's Prayer, and the Sermon on the Mount.

Dodson and Sullivan went to the Detroit meeting with the intention of getting a similar statement approved by the convention, thus rendering humanism a peripheral minority within the American Unitarian Association. However, Dietrich's speech was very powerful, while the strident tone of Sullivan's speech and its insulting remarks about the humanists offended many. As a result the Dodson-Sullivan group lost support and decided not to present their statement to the convention after all.

In his speech, Dietrich said that the power of Christianity was not "the pathetic tale of the life of Jesus, nor the tragic story of his death; no, nor the innocent myth of his triumphant resurrection." It was, rather, the faith of the early Christians in the coming of the kingdom of God that gave their religion its power. In the same way, he said, our faith that the world can be changed is what empowers Unitarians. In *American Religious Humanism*, Mason Olds writes of Dietrich's speech,

> He sounded like an ancient biblical prophet when he proclaimed that the world does not need an ecclesiastical religion, it does not need more priests and prayers and holy

books, it does not need literary essays on academic subjects; but it does need the voice of the prophet going up and down the land, crying "prepare ye the way of mankind and make its way straight."

Dietrich had brilliantly transformed the idea of the common faith, which Dodson said was faith in God, into faith in what he called the Commonwealth of Man. He changed the common faith from a matter of belief in a supernatural power to belief in the ability of human beings to create a better world by their own efforts. And thus he made the transformation of society—not supernaturalism, prayer, and ritual—the cornerstone of Unitarian religion. In so doing, he won the support of the young theistic Unitarian social gospel advocates.

The humanism-theism controversy was not over, but the opportunity for the theists to pass a resolution committing Unitarianism to belief in God had passed. Unitarianism was able to remain a noncreedal religion and to keep the door open to religious humanism.

Meanwhile, the number of religious humanists was growing. Early in the twentieth century, Professor Frank Carlton Doan of Meadville Theological School, the Unitarian seminary, had proclaimed what he called "cosmic humanism." Though somewhat theistic, cosmic humanism insisted on beginning with humankind in the search for the divine. Doan influenced three Meadville graduates who were to become leading humanist spokespersons: J. A. C. Fagginer Auer, Charles Lyttle, and E. Burdette Backus.

When Meadville moved to Chicago in 1926, its students were exposed to the liberal professors at the University of Chicago, including humanist professor of comparative religion and Unitarian A. Eustace Haydon. Another was theologian George Burnham Foster, whose radical thought influenced Haydon, Reese, and Dietrich, as well as others. Some of the leading humanist ministers came out of Meadville in the 1920s and 1930s, including Edwin H. Wilson and Raymond Bragg.

An excellent sense of the religious humanism of the time can be found in the 1927 volume *Humanist Sermons*, edited by Curtis Reese. In his preface, Reese lists three defining beliefs of the new religion. First, humanism affirms "that human life is of supreme worth" and that human beings are ends in themselves, not a means to any other goal. Second, humanism is committed to "human inquiry" as a means of "understanding human experience." This is meant to be a rejection of divine revelation and an affirmation of reason and scientific method. And third, humanism represents the most complete "effort to enrich human experience."

The Humanist Manifesto

In 1933, some of the members of the new Humanist Fellowship, a recently organized group of University of Chicago and Meadville students, suggested there ought to be a summary statement of religious humanism. They asked Roy Wood Sellars to draft such a statement. He did so and called it "a humanist manifesto." Raymond Bragg, Curtis Reese, A. Eustace Haydon, and Edwin H. Wilson revised and edited it for publication. The Manifesto was widely circulated and read and created no little controversy.

Thirty-four people, all men, signed the Manifesto. A number were philosophers, including famous names like John Dewey, John Herman Randall Jr., Roy Wood Sellars, and Edwin A. Burtt. Haydon and another historian of religion, J. A. C. Fagginer Auer of Harvard Divinity School, signed it. So did fifteen Unitarian ministers, including Dietrich, Reese, Bragg, Wilson, Lester Mondale, E. Burdette Backus, Charles Francis Potter, and David Rhys Williams. Clinton Lee Scott was the only Universalist minister to sign it, along with one Jewish rabbi.

The Manifesto actually came at a time when religious humanism had begun to decline after the heady days of the 1920s. The Great Depression turned people's attention to more practical concerns. As William F. Schulz explains,

The skeptical metaphysical speculations in which the humanists engaged were not ones that provided the kind of cosmic assurance an economically insecure people thought they required in a religion. Neither Christian liberalism nor an amorphous adolescent humanism appeared to be able to meet those needs.

Nevertheless, the Manifesto was the quintessential statement of the religious humanism of that period. Bold and forthright, it was clearly intended to proclaim a vital new religious alternative for the twentieth century. The Manifesto begins by proclaiming the birth of a new and viable religion for the modern age:

> The time has come for widespread recognition of the radical changes in religious beliefs throughout the modern world. The time is past for mere revision of traditional attitudes. Science and economic change have disrupted the old beliefs. Religions the world over are under the necessity of coming to terms with new conditions created by a vastly increased knowledge and experience. In every field of human activity, the vital movement is now in the direction of a candid and explicit humanism.

Thus the purpose of the Manifesto, the writers said, was to understand religious humanism better. But in addition to its educational and public relations purpose, it also includes statements with political and economic implications.

The Manifesto points to the danger of religion being identified with the outmoded beliefs of another era. It insists that religious beliefs must be compatible with both the method and the discoveries of modern science. But it also argues that religion has been and must continue to be the means for realizing the highest goals and values of life. Claiming that these reasons make religious humanism imperative for today's world, the Manifesto then sets forth fifteen beliefs or convictions of religious humanism.

The Manifesto asserts that "religious humanists regard the universe as self-existing and not created" and that humans evolved as part of nature in a continuous process. This is clearly a repudiation of theism, a rejection of the literal understanding of the biblical story of the creation of human beings, and an affirmation of biological evolution. The Manifesto also rejects the notion that we are immortal souls residing in a transient physical body.

It also affirms religion and human culture as human creations, and it regards the individual as largely shaped by the culture into which he or she is born. This is a rejection of the idea that religion is based on the revelation of God, affirming instead that it developed and changed over the course of human history like all other aspects of culture.

Maintaining that the universe as depicted by modern science "makes unacceptable any supernatural or cosmic guarantees of human values," the Manifesto holds that values must be determined "by means of intelligent inquiry and by the assessment of their relation to human needs." And it repudiates the idea of divine revelation by insisting that "religion must formulate its hopes and plans in the light of the scientific spirit and method."

The Manifesto defines religion as consisting of "those actions, purposes, and experiences which are humanly significant. Nothing human is alien to the religious. It includes labor, art, science, philosophy, love, friendship, recreation—all that is in its degree expressive of intelligently satisfying human living." Rejecting the distinction between the sacred and the secular, it holds that religion is not a separate compartment of life but a dimension of all of life, a part of who we are and everything we do.

But religious humanism is not only a matter of rejecting supernatural religion and its doctrines. It is even more a matter of affirming human goals, both personal and social. "Religious humanism considers the complete realization of human personality to be the end of man's life and seeks its development and fulfillment in the here and now. This is the explanation of the humanist's social passion."

Rather than "the old attitudes involved in worship and prayer," the ninth thesis declares that "the humanist finds his religious emotions expressed in a heightened sense of personal life and in a cooperative effort to promote social well-being." Traditionally there have been at least three kinds of religious expression: the personal, the priestly, and the prophetic. Personal religion emphasizes the individual's spiritual growth; priestly religion stresses ritual, ceremony, and purification, with corporate worship as the primary means to that end; prophetic religion, without entirely repudiating the importance of the other types, emphasizes ethical living and social transformation. In this thesis, the writers identify religious humanism with the personal and the prophetic traditions and leave little, if any, place for the priestly.

The tenth thesis reads, "It follows that there will be no uniquely religious emotions and attitudes of the kind hitherto associated with belief in the supernatural." Sellars said the importance of theses nine and ten "lies in altering the framework and outward character of religion. They propose a shift from supernaturalism to naturalism, from heaven to earth; with this new emphasis will come new attitudes, aims and procedures. Prayer, for example, rather than being petitionary, will be meditative."

Affirming that religion must promote joy in living, creativity, and "achievements that add to the satisfactions of life," the Manifesto calls for associations and institutions to work for the enhancement of human life. Religious institutions, it says, must be "reconstituted" so that they may function more effectively in the modern world.

The fourteenth thesis criticizes the capitalist system by saying that the "profit-motivated society" is "inadequate" and calling instead for a "socialized and cooperative" economy. The goal was a more equitable distribution of wealth, but the invocation of socialism led to later criticism. However, during the Depression it did seem evident to many that capitalism was not working very well.

The last thesis is one of the Manifesto's finer statements:

> We assert that humanism will (a) affirm life rather than deny it; (b) seek to elicit the possibilities of life, not flee from it; and

(c) endeavor to establish the conditions of a satisfactory life for all, not merely for the few. By this positive morale and intention, humanism will be guided, and from this perspective and alignment the techniques and efforts of humanism will flow.

The Manifesto concludes with these words:

Though we consider the religious forms and ideas of our fathers no longer adequate, the quest for the good life is still the central task for mankind. Man is at last becoming aware that he alone is responsible for the realization of the world of his dreams, that he has within himself the power for its achievement. He must set intelligence and will to the task.

Thus did the writers deliberately seek to change the nature of religion from supernaturalism to naturalism, from heaven to earth, from personal piety to social responsibility.

Publication of the Manifesto set off a flurry of responses. *The Christian Century*, a fairly liberal nondenominational journal, attacked the Manifesto's religion because it was atheistic. While agreeing with some of its social statements, the journal expressed doubt that the Manifesto's social goals could be realized without a theistic grounding. Nevertheless, with the Manifesto, religious humanism went public as a viable religious option for those for whom the beliefs, myths, and symbols of Judaism and Christianity were no longer believable and had lost their power. It represented the emergence of a new religion in America, a religion that would find its ecclesiastical home in Unitarianism and Universalism.

In the years since the publication of the Manifesto, humanist organizations have been formed in many countries. Examples include the American Humanist Association, the British Humanist Association, the Canadian Humanist Association, the Society for Humanistic Judaism, and humanist organizations in Norway, Holland, Australia, Korea, and India. There is also an International Humanist and Ethical Union. Most of these groups consider themselves secular rather than religious humanists. The major ex-

ceptions are Humanistic Judaism and "HUUmanists," formerly
the Fellowship of Religious Humanists, a group affiliated with the
Unitarian Universalist Association.

Weaknesses

The religious humanism of this pre-World War II period had several
serious drawbacks. For one thing, it was highly individualistic. The
independent, autonomous individual was the ideal. Thus it lacked
an emphasis on community and said nothing about the church.

It also exemplified no sense of the tragic, of the place of pain
and suffering, loss and grief, death and dying. It seemed to take an
attitude of indifference toward the harsh realities of human life.
John Dietrich's ministry illustrates this point. Dietrich had almost
no pastoral ministry and did not normally call on members who
were hospitalized. When asked why he did not call on sick members, Dietrich replied with the stoic comment that they would
have to learn to cope with their problems themselves.

Humanism during this period placed too much emphasis on
reason and ignored the emotional or feeling aspect of the self. It
emphasized the mind and virtually ignored the heart. It also
lacked a sense of openness to mystery and the unknown. It was
naively optimistic in thinking that the unknown is simply that
which science is not yet able to understand.

In addition, the first Manifesto showed no awareness of the
extent and depth of evil in the world. The Manifesto made no
mention of human freedom but instead seemed to affirm a cultural
determinism in which the individual is the product of the social
environment. Without an understanding of the human capacity
for free choice, it is not possible to account for evil.

And finally, the humanism of this time was too dogmatic and
seemingly intolerant of other perspectives, especially theism.

Despite its weaknesses, the Humanist Manifesto of 1933 was
an important statement of an early and evolving religious humanism, laying the foundation for humanism's ongoing development.

Changes and Challenges

MUCH HAS CHANGED in the seventy plus years since the Manifesto. We have gone through a depression, the horrors of a world war, the Holocaust and the Soviet Gulag, a cold war and a terrorist attack, decreasing our optimism and increasing our tragic sense of life. We have been deeply affected by the feminist movement, the environmental crisis and the new romanticism, called postmodernism, which questions Enlightenment assumptions. Moreover, the resurgence of evangelical Christianity has moved our society's religious perspective in a conservative direction. These factors have led in recent years to a decline in religious humanism as many people felt that religious humanism was overly rational and lacked a spiritual dimension. If it is to thrive in the twenty-first century, religious humanism needs to engage in deeper thinking and find a richer language.

However, by the time of the merger of the Unitarian and Universalist churches in 1961, religious humanism had replaced liberal theism as the ideological center of the new Unitarian Universalist Association. In numerous surveys in the 1970s and 1980s, well over half the members of Unitarian Universalist churches checked humanism as best describing their religious perspective. The theists, and particularly the Unitarian Universalist Christians, were now the ones who questioned whether they belonged to this religious association. As often happens, however, a rigid humanist orthodoxy developed. In a 1997 article in *First Days Record* Richard Erhardt remembers,

> From our inception (in 1961) to the present any right think-ing Unitarian Universalist leaned toward humanistic under-standings of the world. When I was growing up I learned that it was all right to say just about anything that was on my mind in my UU congregation. But that right ended if I men-tioned the word God. That right ended if I pondered an af-terlife. That right ended if I ventured out of Newtonian physics toward the quantum models and its implications which strongly point away from a modernistic humanism toward a post-modern understanding of life. I had experi-enced an understanding of humanism as orthodoxy.

Religious humanism, which had once championed freedom of belief, had now become all too often entrenched, parochial, and illiberal. In place of challenging the attempts of others to petrify Unitarian Universalism into a Christian or theistic orthodoxy, hu-manism had itself become the ossified orthodoxy. This humanist orthodoxy did the cause of Unitarian Universalist humanism a good deal of harm. Many of the old-guard humanists were rigid thinkers who defined humanism too narrowly and did not wel-come those who did not fully agree with them. Their philosophy was shaped by positivism and rational empiricism. It was a blood-less, passionless religious philosophy, and while it articulated hu-manism effectively for several decades, the times changed and the old humanism did not.

I experienced that kind of humanism as a twenty-two-year-old first-year seminary student. I knew I did not belong in the Southern Baptist denomination, and so I visited a Unitarian church. No one greeted me going in or coming out; I heard a thought-provoking sermon and some interesting readings, but not much else happened in the service. It was a fine intellectual ex-perience, but it was cold and unfriendly, and as a result I was lost to Unitarian Universalism for another twenty years. That kind of humanism diminished the vitality of Unitarian Universalist religious humanism. A number of Unitarian Universalist humanists in recent years have complained about feeling under siege as a result of the increased popularity of theism. At the 1997 General Assembly, the Fellowship of Religious Humanists hosted a workshop dealing with the question of whether humanists could really stay in Unitarian Universalism or whether they should leave. Later that year, *UU World* carried an article about Unitarian Universalist humanism entitled "The Marginalized Majority." It seems that traditional humanism has lost much of its appeal. The recent Commission on Appraisal survey and report, *Engaging Our Theological Diversity*, suggests that while the vast majority of Unitarian Universalists do not espouse supernaturalism and a supernatural deity, a large percentage affirm the use of God language to express their convictions.

Unitarian Universalist Theism

The traditional meaning of *theism* is belief in a deity who is personal, supernatural, and separate from the world. The kind of theism many Unitarian Universalists affirm is a form of naturalistic theism in which God is understood as part of the natural universe rather than a supernatural being, and is immanent rather than transcendent. Whether this God is a personal being or an impersonal force is a matter of interpretation. Often it is not clear which kind of God is meant. There is a very thin line between this naturalistic theism and religious humanism. Thus, ministers who talk about God as the life force, the power of creativity, or the power of life and love within us are very close to humanistic naturalism.

The Reverend Scott Alexander, senior minister of River Road Unitarian Church in Bethesda, Maryland, proclaims, "I proudly and passionately call myself a humanist." But he also calls himself a "naturalistic, mystical theist" because he believes that something he calls the spirit of God is animating the world and all living beings. He experiences this spirit of God as a "powerful spiritual presence . . . of love, decency, joyfulness, and hope." But he does not regard God as a supernatural, authoritarian deity.

I believe that expresses quite well the kind of theism that a large number of Unitarian Universalists affirm. It is a sister to humanistic religious naturalism, inasmuch as it is both naturalistic and affirming of humanistic values. Rather than feeling marginalized, religious humanists should rejoice because this naturalistic theism is much closer to what they believe than traditional theism is. The heart of humanism should not be what we reject but what we affirm. Both theistic and nontheistic religious naturalism affirm the dignity and worth of each person, the importance of reason and experience in making judgments, dedication to the well-being of all people, and an affirmation of the authority of *human* experience.

But the difference between this kind of naturalistic theism and humanistic naturalism is more than semantic. I suspect that those who agree with most of the tenets of humanism but retain a sense of deity are simply reluctant to give up belief in an ultimate ground of being that is in some sense spiritual. Some might call this unwillingness a failure of nerve, a lack of courage to go it alone in an empty universe, while others would argue that naturalistic theists are simply seeking something deeper than what they have found in religious humanism. Grounding humanism in religious naturalism may provide the depth that they have not found in the older humanism.

Humanist Manifesto II

In 1973 a new generation of humanists, as well as some of the signers of the first Manifesto who were still living, signed Humanist Manifesto II. Drafted by philosopher Paul Kurtz and Unitarian Universalist minister Edwin Wilson, it attempted to correct some of the flaws of the first Manifesto. While it does not directly address the problem of humanist orthodoxy in Unitarian Universalism or argue for humanism as a religion, as the first Manifesto did, it does illustrate some of the changes in humanist thinking that occurred over the forty years since the first Manifesto.

The second Manifesto begins by admitting that the first Manifesto had been too optimistic, citing the horrible atrocities of Nazism and the suppression of human rights by other totalitarian regimes. It notes that science has been the source of hideous evil as well as great good. Nevertheless, it reaffirms the earlier Manifesto's rejection of supernaturalism and offers humanism as a hopeful vision of the future. It tempers the optimism of the first Manifesto by recognizing the future dangers of ecological destruction, overpopulation, totalitarianism and nuclear or biochemical catastrophe. The second Manifesto reaffirms reason and the scientific method but also insists that if humanity is to survive,

> We need to extend the uses of scientific method, not renounce them, to fuse reason with compassion in order to build constructive social and moral values . . . . The ultimate goal should be the fulfillment of the potential for growth in each human personality—not for the favored few but for all of humankind.

Humanist Manifesto II suggests that at its best, "religion may inspire dedication to the highest ethical ideals," but goes on to repudiate traditional dogmatic and authoritarian religions. On the subject of ethics, it asserts that moral values have their source in human experience and need no theological sanction. Insisting on the effectiveness of reason and intelligence, it cautions against regarding them as independent of or in opposition to emotion.

The next section proclaims the dignity of the individual person as a central humanist value. It condemns exploitative sexual behavior and supports the development of a responsible attitude toward sexuality. The rest of the document affirms "the full range of civil liberties," an "open and democratic society," separation of church and state, social justice, and "elimination of all discrimination based on race, religion, sex, age or national origin." It urges nonviolent means of settling international disputes and calls for international cooperation to reduce the threat to the environment. Humanist Manifesto II was signed by a number of well-known scientists, philosophers, and Unitarian Universalist ministers. The youngest signer was William F. Schulz, then a student at Meadville Lombard Theological School, who later served two terms as president of the Unitarian Universalist Association. From today's perspective, it is an improvement in many ways over the first Manifesto. It corrects some of the problems of the first and addresses some of the issues, such as environmental concerns and feminism, that emerged after the first Manifesto was written. It describes a more open and less dogmatic humanism. However, it does not do justice to the religious and spiritual dimension nor does it provide an adequate understanding of human evil or the role of the emotions.

Humanist Manifesto III

Recognizing the need to continue to restate humanist principles, the leaders of the American Humanist Association drafted a third Manifesto entitled "Humanism and Its Aspirations"in 2003. It consists of six theses along with a short prologue and epilogue. It identifies humanism as a "progressive philosophy of life" rather than a religious expression. In fact, it does not use the word *religion* at all, but eleven Unitarian Universalist ministers, including myself, were among the eighty-nine original signers. Among the many scientists who signed the third Manifesto were twenty Nobel laureates.

Humanist Manifesto III reaffirms the central tenets of humanism, including the understanding that human beings are "an integral part of nature, the result of unguided evolutionary change" and that our "knowledge of the world is derived by observation, experimentation and rational analysis." It regards ethical values as the result of "human need and interest," and suggests that humanists are "guided by reason, inspired by compassion and informed by experience." Affirming the social nature of human life and the value of relationships, it emphasizes the importance of "service to humane ideals" and maintains that "working to benefit society" is the path to happiness. The epilogue includes a commitment to "protect nature's integrity, diversity and beauty in a secure, sustainable manner."

"Humanism and Its Aspirations" is a fine short statement of a current humanist philosophy. It hints at some of the needed changes in the humanist perspective without spelling these out in detail. The mention of environmental responsibility, the use of the words *compassion* and *diversity* and several other statements add to its power and timeliness. Happily, the document does not have a dogmatic or strident tone, nor is it overly optimistic. However, it too makes no mention of the religious/spiritual dimension and says nothing about the depth and pervasiveness of human evil.

Functional Ultimacy

One of the criticisms theists often level at humanism is that it deifies humankind or makes humankind ultimate. Unitarian Universalist William R. Jones of Florida State University offers a compelling defense. He concedes that we are not "ontologically ultimate," that is, we did not create ourselves. However, he suggests that we have no recourse but to function as though we are ultimate in that we must create our own values and we must decide for ourselves what is true and what criteria we use to make those decisions. Jones illustrates this point with the biblical story of Abraham. When Abraham believes God has told him to sacrifice his only son, he prepares to do so. But at the last minute, he believes God has told him to kill a ram instead. Both times, Abraham has to decide whether what he believes to be the command of God actually comes from God or from the pagan deity Moloch, who requires the sacrifice of the firstborn. Abraham functions as the moral ultimate, since he alone has to decide what is right. Similarly, the theist of today must decide whether what she believes to be God's will is truly God's will or is simply the result of her own thinking or preference. Thus there is no difference between the humanist and the theist in this respect.

Jones also insists that it is freedom rather than reason that is at the heart of humanism, and this freedom is finite or limited freedom rather than absolute freedom.

Jones' understanding of functional ultimacy answers the critics who say that humanism makes humankind divine, and his concept of freedom answers the critics who say that humanism gives humankind absolute freedom.

Feminism

The women's movement has contributed a great deal to our understanding of what it means to be human, and religious humanism needs to incorporate feminist insights into its worldview.

Rebecca Parker suggests three possible contributions of the women's movement to religious humanism. First, feminism reminds us that we are mind/body beings, and we need to take bodily existence seriously. We must recognize that the self is not a disembodied mind or intellect and incorporate feelings such as pain, anger, and joy into our perspective. Traditional religious humanism, however, emphasizes reason and the intellect to the near exclusion of the body and the emotions.

The women's movement also teaches us, according to Parker, that we are not independent individuals but interdependent and interconnected with all other human beings and all life. Our lives touch other lives, and other lives touch us. To be fully human is to be in relationship. Traditional religious humanism tends to prioritize the individual at the expense of valuing the connections among people and with all of life.

Another contribution of the women's movement is increased awareness that human beings are capable of being profoundly hurt. We are vulnerable and woundable. Religious humanists need to pay more attention to the pain that many people experience and to ways in which we can minister to people in pain. The stoic tendency of John Dietrich's brand of humanism is not helpful to those who are hurting. The role of humanist ministers and congregations, as it is for all religious people, is to be present with those who are suffering, to listen to their concerns, and to offer comfort that is honest and loving. Often there is no rational explanation as to why good people suffer, but it is important that people in pain know that others care about them enough to spend quality time with them. Human presence and human touching are often more helpful than words at such times.

These are areas the older humanism did not really deal with. If religious humanism is to remain a viable religious alternative, it must incorporate these understandings.

The Environmental Movement

Religious humanism has been criticized for being too anthropocentric. By placing human concerns and values at the center of its ethic, the critics say, humanism treats nature simply as something to be used for the benefit of humankind. The old humanism was even considered one of the value systems responsible for the many years of damage to the environment. We need to make environmental concerns an integral part of our perspective. The need to save and protect our environment is urgent, and religious humanism needs to address this in order to stay relevant in today's world.

Postmodernism

Perhaps the most significant influence on humanism today is the philosophy of postmodernism, which criticizes the modern approach to reality that arose in the Enlightenment era—the approach that provided the worldview and epistemological basis for traditional forms of humanism. This modern worldview regarded the world as knowable through reason and the scientific method and as having universal and objective truths. It believed in progress by applying science to human and social problems.

Postmodern thinkers seek to deconstruct or tear down this modern worldview.

Postmodernism permeates our culture. As Hegel said, "The owl of Minerva comes out only after the shades of night have fallen." That is, philosophy does not shape the culture, it reflects it. We need to understand postmodernism because, as Michael Werner puts it, "These are the assumptions, unchallenged premises of our culture that permeate everything in our lives. These premises mold all our thinking as individuals, dictate the nature of our society, and indeed mold our religious thinking as religious liberals."

Instead of emphasizing reason and cognition, postmodernism stresses intuition and the mystical. Rather than individualism and competition, it emphasizes the community and cooperation. In the postmodern way of thinking, people make value judgments about what is right or wrong on the basis of whether or not something feels okay, not on the basis of reasoned argument about the benefit to people. Postmodernism also says that everything is relative and a matter of one's own perspective. It has no other grounds for determining what is right or wrong, good or bad.

Postmodernism also maintains that all our ideas of truth and our basic sense of reality are social constructions, that what we call reality has actually been constructed over thousands of years of human history. Postmodernism says that there is no basis in objective reality for our values and beliefs, and that reason itself is often nothing more than a form of rationalization that is used to gain power or control.

Traditionally, humanism has been tied to the modernist way of thinking, but it does not need to be. Religious humanism can benefit by acknowledging some of the postmodern temperament and worldview. However, whereas both modernism and postmodernism are extreme positions, a new religious humanism can incorporate the best of each. Postmodernism can help us understand our own prejudices and give us a greater humility about our beliefs. It can teach us to listen to what our intuition and emotional experience tell us. It can provide an antidote to traditional religious humanism's tendency to be dogmatic, overly rational, and strictly individualistic. But that does not mean we have to repudiate reason and critical thinking. As we shall see, the perspective I am calling humanistic religious naturalism can integrate many postmodern ideas with the best of the modern worldview.

A Postsecular World?

It is becoming increasingly apparent that interest in religion is once again in the ascendancy in this country. Evangelical Christianity has been increasing in numbers and influence for several decades. An interest in "spirituality" began to be expressed among Unitarian Universalists and many unchurched people in the 1970s and 1980s. The "New Age" movement also represents an interest in religiosity. The number of books dealing with religious, quasi-religious, and spiritual topics has increased substantially in recent years. Beginning with the first Great Awakening, America has repeatedly experienced periods of great religious interest. It seems that in periods of change, uncertainty, and insecurity, many in this country turn to religion.

Much of this resurgence of interest in religion is occurring among people who have no religious background and no commitment to the traditional religions. This situation creates an opportunity for a vital religious humanism. If religious humanism is to be a viable alternative for these people, I believe it must develop and embrace a nontheistic understanding of spirituality and a meaningful concept of religion. Many people are seeking a religious perspective that incorporates the discoveries of modern science but turns away from stories, myths, and symbols that, for them, have lost their power.

Feminism, the environmental movement, and postmodernism can provide correctives to some of the failings of an earlier religious humanism and humanist orthodoxy. The succeeding chapters will incorporate these and other themes into a vital and viable theology of humanistic religious naturalism.

Anchored in Nature

AS WE HAVE become more aware of the unimaginable vastness of the universe and the beauty, importance, and fragility of the natural world, to even imply that humankind is the center of all things is increasingly problematic, not to mention presumptuous and arrogant. On the contrary, we have become more aware of how small and insignificant we human beings are in the larger scheme of things. Medieval theologians referred to this awareness as looking at things *sub specie aeternitatis*—literally, "under the aspect of eternity."

I regard that larger perspective as both humbling and healthy, and therefore I believe it is important to conceive of religious humanism within the broader context of religious naturalism, one of the most exciting developments in religious thinking in the last century. The last few decades in particular have seen a resurgence in interest in this theology. A group called Unitarian Universalist Religious Naturalists, of which I am a member, was formed in 2004.

Naturalism is a philosophical perspective that denies the existence of the supernatural and maintains that there is only one realm, the natural universe. Thus, metaphysically, it is monistic rather than dualistic, affirming one reality rather than two. Humanism has always been naturalistic, but it has not made explicit the religious implications of that perspective.

Religious naturalism finds religious meaning in the natural world. Its proponents include such philosophers as Spinoza, George Santayana, and John Dewey, and theologians such as Henry Nelson Wieman, Bernard Meland, Bernard Loomer, Frederick May Eliot, and others. My own perspective belongs to the larger tradition of religious naturalism, but is nontheistic.

Jerome Stone's definition of religious naturalism is helpful:

> Negatively it asserts that there seems to be no ontologically distinct and superior realm (such as God, soul, or heaven) to ground, explain, or give meaning to this world. Positively it affirms that attention should be focused on this world to provide whatever explanation and meaning are possible to this life. Now religious naturalism is a variety of naturalism which involves a set of beliefs and attitudes that there are religious aspects of this world which can be appreciated within a naturalistic framework.

For naturalists, the natural universe is ultimate. It is the ground of our being, that in which we live and move and upon which we depend for our very existence. Nature refers to the totality of things in the universe, but we can experience it only in bits and pieces, never as a whole, except perhaps through our thinking and imaginative processes. Donald Crosby writes that "nature is the whole system of things and relations that continues to give rise to new particular things and types of things, maintains them in being as long as they exist, and makes possible their distinctive traits." John Ruskin Clark calls it "the great living system." However it is defined, the natural realm is, in a naturalistic perspective, the ultimate ground of being and meaning.

Philosopher Rem Edwards identifies six characteristics of naturalism in *Reason and Religion*, of which the following four are applicable to our discussion:

~ Only nature exists and by implication . . . the supernatural does not exist. By nature is meant "the spatio-temporal universe as a whole existing independently of knowing mind."

~ Nature as a whole is nonpersonal. . . . whatever order there is within nature is inherent and was not introduced by any sort of intelligence of cosmic proportions.

~ Nature as a whole, including the basic stuff within it, is eternal and necessary in the sense of being uncreated, indestructible, and self-sufficient.

~ All natural events have causes that are themselves natural events.

By affirming that nature is impersonal, naturalism opposes the Judeo-Christian idea of a personal deity. By regarding nature as eternal and all that exists, it rejects the notion that the cosmos is dependent on some other power for its existence. Nothing is caused by something outside of nature. Naturalism also affirms that nature has always existed and always will although it changes form.

Naturalism maintains that human beings are products of nature and natural causes. We are simply one of a prolific nature's multitudinous creations, each unique and special, and all part of one interdependent web. Naturalism also rejects the idea that a human being consists of a separate entity called mind or soul or spirit temporarily dwelling in a physical body. Instead, naturalists believe in the unity of the mind and body, which means that there is no life of the individual after physical death. This acceptance of human mortality and transience leads religious naturalists to feel gratitude for life and a commitment to make the one life we have as meaningful and as joyful as possible.

In addition to avoiding anthropocentrism, religious naturalism provides a deeper and richer perspective than classical humanism, and it also affirms a positive relationship with science. Since the time of Copernicus and Galileo scientific discoveries have posed a challenge to religious beliefs in the West. Modern science brought new understandings of the world and of the nature of humankind, some of which called into question the traditional worldview of religion. Religious thinkers have responded in one of three ways. The first of these has been outright opposition to the scientific discoveries and the scientific worldview by religion. This is the position usually taken by conservative religions, as we see, for example, in evangelical Christianity's rejection of biological evolution and the evidence for global warming. The second type of relationship between religion and science is sometimes called *parallelism*, since it asserts that science and religion deal with two different ways of looking at the world, each of which has validity but which do not intersect. In this view, religion deals with questions of the meaning and purpose of life whereas science deals with the physical nature of things. Put differently, religion is concerned with matters of the spirit while science addresses issues related to the material world. This is the perspective taken by many moderate to liberal Christian theologians. The third type of relationship, that affirmed by religious naturalism, regards religion and science as in a dialogue in which a dynamic religion is constantly learning from science, evolving new understandings in the process and resulting in a scientifically informed religious perspective.

A Sense of Wonder

With its emphasis on reason and the intellect, traditional religious humanism has little place for such qualities as awe and reverence. Anchoring religious humanism in religious naturalism gives it a deeper, richer, and more meaningful dimension.

This deeper dimension is articulated in the Unitarian Universalist Religious Naturalists' brochure:

> We find our sources of meaning within the natural world, where humans are understood to be emergent from and hence a part of nature. Our religious quest is informed and guided by the deepening and evolving understandings fostered by scientific inquiry. It is also informed and guided by the mindful understandings inherent in our human traditions, including art, literature, philosophy, and the religions of the world.
>
> The natural world and its emergent manifestations in human creativity and community are the focus of our im-

mersion, wonder, and reverence, and our common naturalistic orientation generates our shared sense of place, gratitude and joy.

For many people, myself included, nature evokes some of the
same feelings that a supernatural deity evokes in the adherents of
traditional religion. For me, the unimaginable vastness of the universe and the incredible complexity of life evoke awe and reverence greater than anything I experienced as a theist. I am struck
with wonder and amazement at the fact that there are some one
hundred billion galaxies in the universe, each with about one hundred billion stars (more than all the grains of sand on all the
beaches of the world, according to Carl Sagan) and at the fact that
the universe is about fifteen billion years old. I am filled with reverence and astonishment to know that there are some thirty million different species in the world and that all life evolved over
billions of years from one-celled organisms and that our human
species has been evolving for millions of years from a common ancestor we share with other primates. I am overcome with amazement at the thought that my body consists of ten trillion cells and
that my brain contains about one hundred billion neurons and one
hundred trillion synapses.

I feel wonder and amazement at nature's majesty, beauty,
complexity, and power. I feel joy and comfort among its trees or
by its water, and refreshed and rejuvenated from working in its soil
or walking in its woods. I feel reverence when I ponder the in-
comprehensible vastness of the universe and the equally mind-
boggling smallness of the submicroscopic world. That the
universe is, to quote the title of a book by physicist Freeman
Dyson, "infinite in all directions" is beyond my ability to imagine.

Even the immense power of nature as exemplified in earthquakes, hurricanes, tsunamis, and tornadoes is a source of awe.
That nature's power can destroy human beings and human creations is reason for great sorrow, but it is not the result of malice,
and certainly not "the will of God" as is sometimes said. We can use
our ingenuity and creativity to do all we can to protect ourselves

from nature's destructive power, but we will never be entirely successful. Nature is like the Hindu godhead that consists of the creator (Brahma), the preserver (Vishnu), and the destroyer (Shiva). For many religious naturalists, the experience of nature, both beneficial and destructive, evokes a sense of the unity of all things. They think of themselves as "nature mystics," practitioners of a mysticism devoid of supernaturalism.

Emerson and the Transcendentalists saw nature as being rich in aesthetic, moral, and religious values. At the beginning of his great essay "Nature," Emerson recommends looking up with wonder and delight at the stars and adds, "The stars awaken a certain reverence, because though always present, they are inaccessible; but all natural objects make kindred impression, when the mind is open to their influence." This is of course the same Emerson who, like many today, experienced a greater sense of reverence by walking in the woods than he found in church:

> In the woods, we return to reason and faith. There I find that nothing can befall me in life—no disgrace, no calamity . . . which nature cannot repair. Standing on the bare ground— my head bathed by the blithe air and lifted into infinite space—all mean egotism vanishes.

For religious naturalists, living in a natural environment is a spiritual experience. Freed from supernaturalism, the religious naturalist can be devoted to a nature that nurtures and sustains. It is not incidental that people speak of "Mother Earth." Our ties to nature are deep and intimate.

A Religious Story

Every religious vision needs to be anchored in a story that provides an account of how the world came into being, the place of human beings, and the meaning and direction of life, especially human life. The traditional stories that have sustained Western culture for several millennia are no longer efficacious, but modern science has given us a new story with multiple layers of rich meaning.

In an important essay, "Toward a Humanist Vocabulary of Reverence," David Bumbaugh argues that humanism has been in decline because it has lacked a "language of reverence," but he finds such a language in humankind's relationship to nature, especially as we have come to know it through modern evolutionary science. He notes that the more we understand the magnificence of the universe, the more we stand in reverence before its mystery:

> When the Humanist Manifesto declared that we are part of nature and we have emerged as the result of a continuous process . . . it gave us an immensely richer, longer, more complex history, one rooted in a system which invites not blind faith but challenge and correction and amendment, one which embraces "truth known or to be known." It also gave us a language of reverence because it provides a story rooted not in the history of a single tribe or a particular people, but a history rooted in the sum of our knowledge of the universe itself. It gave us a doctrine of incarnation which suggests not that the holy became human in one place at one time to convey a special message to a single chosen people, but that the universe itself is continually incarnating itself in microbes and maples, in hummingbirds and human beings, constantly inviting us to tease out the revelation contained in stars and atoms and every living thing. A language of reverence for Humanists begins with our understanding of this story as a religious story—a vision of reality that contains within it the sources of a moral, ethical, transcendent self-understanding.

Bumbaugh goes on to suggest that this story is a religious story because it calls us out of our little self-centered worlds and enables us to see ourselves as part of the great living system we call the cosmos. He suggests that this story gives a larger meaning and a broader ethic to our lives. For the religious naturalist, as well as the religious humanist, our connection to nature is a profound spiritual experience that evokes awe, wonder, and reverence.

I concur with Bumbaugh, for I believe that religions need stories to provide a mythic core that offers a vision of ultimate reality. I believe the epic of cosmic evolution is the narrative that underlies humanistic religious naturalism and that provides the individual with a meaningful worldview and a sense of belonging to a larger process. The epic of cosmic evolution that begins with the Big Bang provides us with a vision of the universe as a single reality, one long spectacular process of change and development—an unfolding drama, a universal story for humankind. Like no other story, it humbles us as we contemplate the complexity of the cosmic process, and it amazes us when we try to imagine its magnitude. Like no other story, it evokes reverence as we feel its power, and awe and wonder as we visualize its beauty. Like no other story, it gives us a scientifically based cosmology that tells us how we came to be and what we are made of. As early twentieth-century British biologist Julian Huxley put it, "We are the universe becoming conscious of itself." Like no other story, it teaches us that we are all members of one family sharing the same genetic code and a similar history; it evokes gratitude and astonishment at the gift of life itself and inspires responsible living. Like no other story, it gives meaning and purpose to human beings as the agents responsible for the current and future stages of cultural evolution.

The epic of evolution is "everybody's story," but it is uniquely the story that the religious naturalist claims. It is a story with a scientifically based worldview and values that are both scientific and morally relevant to the human situation. It is a story of the creative powers of matter-energy and of the changing and adaptive powers of living cells. It is a story of the growth and transformation of living beings—of the emergence, in the words of biologist Ursula Goodenough, of "something more out of nothing but." It is our sacred story.

Our story began approximately fourteen billion years ago, when the universe erupted from its unimaginably hot and dense singularity and expanded very rapidly, sending its elementary particles out into the vast unknown. The story continued as the early hydrogen and helium atoms drew together, attracted by gravity.

Those particles slowly began to form galaxies, at least one hundred billion of them in the dark cosmic space, and each galaxy spun out billions of stars. Five billion years after its original explosion, the universe gave birth to the Milky Way galaxy with its ten thousand new stars, including our sun. While the sun was forming, the material surrounding it came together to form planet Earth, comets, and the other planets of the solar system.

Because of the earth's position in the solar system, and because its hot core kept bubbling up into its ocean waters, atoms were able to bond together to form new and different molecules—the building blocks of organic and inorganic matter. The building blocks accumulated in the waters of the earth and formed the "primal soup." Over thousands of years of chemical activity, the first living cell was formed. Amazingly, cellular life emerged from nonlife, empowered by energy from the sun and by the creative ability to self-replicate.

This wonder of evolution continued when mutations changed the genetic instructions for replication, resulting in organisms that varied slightly from their parents. Those organisms that survived through natural selection—the ones that adapted best to their environment—continued to grow and change throughout millions of years. All life on earth has a common ancestor, a single-celled organism from which all humans, as well as all other living organisms, have evolved.

By about six hundred million years ago, multicellular organisms arose—small and simple at first, then larger and more complex. About two hundred million years ago, mammals emerged. Over millions of years they slowly developed the capacity for feelings and emotional sensitivity, the ability to see and enjoy the beauty of the world and to feel fear in the face of its terror. Eventually these qualities deepened into conscious self-awareness.

Four million years ago in Africa, *homo erectus* emerged. These early humans stood upright and, about two million years later, began to make tools and control fire. Some thirty-five thousand years ago, humans depicted their world in cave paintings. About twelve thousand years ago, they began to live in communities, domesticate animals, and grow crops for their food. Some members of the species migrated from Africa to Eurasia, and from there to the Americas and Australia. Communities grew in size and number, leading to urban centers. Their concentrations of wealth and power were protected by a military class with weapons and fortifications.

Language and writing developed, and what we call civilization emerged in somewhat differing forms throughout the planet. For the most part, people were ruled by kings, but democratic city-states developed in Greece. Eventually in Europe, nation states brought together heretofore semi-independent groups under one ruler. As a result of the American and French Revolutions, democratic forms of government began to be adopted by nations, a process still under way.

Evolution has three stages: inorganic, organic, and cultural. The inorganic stage saw the emergence of matter and the formation of galaxies, stars, and planets. In the organic stage, life-forms emerged. This stage culminated in the birth of mind and self-consciousness in human beings. The emergence of mind and consciousness has brought about a qualitative change in the nature of evolution. No longer solely a biological process, evolution is now psychosocial and under the control of the human race. What we do affects the future of life on this planet. This third stage of evolution, the cultural stage, involves moral and spiritual responsibility for the preservation of the earth's resources and for advancement in many areas: social and political justice, the arts, and human understanding through the sciences. This means that we are no longer simply responsible for passing on good genes to our offspring. We now also have a duty to pass along the results of our creative activities. Thus evolution takes on a new twist and creates a new dimension of meaning in our lives.

Our story has several important religious implications. Most importantly, it tells us that we all share a common ancestor. In the words of Brian Swimme and Thomas Berry, "Every living being of Earth is cousin to every other living being." We are all one family, and that suggests that we should be more loving and more tolerant of the diversity of beliefs and perspectives among us. It also implies that we should treat other life-forms with greater respect. We can no longer think of ourselves as separate from the rest of life, for we are all part of one holy global ecosystem. In *The Sacred Depths of Nature*, Ursula Goodenough writes,

> Blessed be the tie that binds. It anchors us. We are embedded in the great evolutionary story of planet Earth, the spare, elegant process of mutation and selection, and bricolage. And this means that we are anything but alone.

Our story provides a firm foundation for a responsible environmental ethic—one based not only on our human need for clean air and water but also on the intrinsic value of the natural world. Traditional humanism has been criticized for valuing the world only as it serves the needs and interests of humans. Humanistic naturalism, on the other hand, clearly regards nature as valuable in and of itself, since nature is the ground of all that is, including humankind.

Symbols play an important role in the way we think and act. Thus the sense of being dependent on a nurturing "Mother Nature" leads to an ethic that emphasizes love, cooperation, caring, and compassion, whereas the concept of a father God tends to result in an ethic that stresses authority, obedience, punishment, and even violence.

Humanistic Religious Naturalism

Having both a religious story or myth and a sense of wonder and reverence toward nature distinguishes religious naturalism from traditional religious humanism. Religious naturalism finds in nature not only the creative source of all life but also a source of experiences that are deeply religious. The romantic poets in particular celebrate this dimension of the naturalistic perspective. William Wordsworth expresses it in this well-known passage from "Lines Composed a Few Miles above Tintern Abbey":

> Therefore am I still
> A lover of the meadows and the woods,
> And mountains; and of all that we behold,
> From this green earth; of all the mighty world
> Of eye, and ear—both what they half-create,
> And what perceive; well-pleased to recognize
> In Nature and the language of the sense,
> The anchor of my purest thoughts, the nurse,
> The guide, the guardian of my heart, and soul
> Of all my moral being.

Religious naturalism provides humanism with both a solid philosophical foundation and an inspiring sacred story. It gives humanism a cosmology, a deeper spiritual dimension, an environmental ethic, and a larger vision. Humanism is greatly enriched by grounding it in religious naturalism. I call this melded theological stance humanistic religious naturalism, and I believe the following fifteen points articulate its essential affirmations:

~ Human beings are of great worth and value—the highest form of life we know. But we are not self-sufficient—we are dependent beings, dependent on nature and natural processes. We are creatures of nature and products of biological evolution.

~ The human body and mind are part of one unified whole. What we call mind and soul and spirit are not separate entities but simply different functions of the brain. Human beings have no conscious survival after death. This life is all there is, and our challenge is to make the most of it.

~ The natural order is all there is as far as we can tell. There is no supernatural order as far as we can know.

~ We can only know what we actually experience with our five senses, plus what we can deduce and induce from that experience through rational mental activity, especially the scientific method.

~ The goal of human beings is to become more fully human. Whatever enriches and enhances human life is good; whatever diminishes human life is evil. Growth is essential to realizing the goal of greater humanness—personal growth, spiritual growth, intellectual growth, moral growth.

~ Since all humans are of inherent worth and dignity, democracy is the best and highest form of social and political organization—democracy understood and practiced as a social system in which every person has equal voice in decision making in government, corporations, and institutions.

~ Education is essential for personal growth and for a democratic society. Education should include learning to think critically, becoming steeped in the methods and discoveries of the modern natural and social sciences, and gaining knowledge of history, philosophy, and the arts.

~ The pursuit of social, economic, and racial justice and the eradication of all forms of exploitation and oppression are central to the vision of a better world.

~ Ethical values and principles do not come from a supernatural source but rather have evolved from millennia of human experience. Reverence for life in all its forms is a central principle in the ethical life. Gratitude for the gift of life and for the many contributions of others to culture is a key motivating factor for ethics as well as an attitude that leads to other virtues.

~ Human beings are not totally determined by nature or nurture but have some degree of genuine freedom of choice, which can be increased by knowledge, education, and critical thinking.

~ Awe and reverence at the incredible universe in which we live and at its remarkable evolutionary history are important aspects of religious experience. The ethical corollary to this includes preservation and protection of our natural environment and nature's resources.

~ Truth, goodness, and beauty are important to the enrichment of human life. The beauty of nature, the arts, architecture, and literature are sources of spiritual value.

~ Human beings have the potential to solve many of the major problems of the world through science, education, cooperation, and a willingness to put the common good ahead of self-interest. Progress, though not inevitable, is possible.

~ A higher standard of living for all people is desirable and possible through a more just and equitable distribution of resources and wealth.

~ It is essential to be open to new ideas, values, and ways of thinking and acting. Therefore one must be willing to question basic assumptions, including one's own.

To those of us for whom the idea of God no longer has relevance, humanistic religious naturalism provides a worldview that retains the best of the Western religious tradition and discards the rest. It offers a new faith that not only fosters our sense of the wonder and significance of life but also promotes a profound perspective on the human condition and a powerful commitment to work for human betterment.

Human Nature and Destiny

In his 1828 sermon, "Likeness to God," William Ellery Channing writes,

> I do and must reverence human nature. Neither the sneers of a worldly skepticism nor the groans of a gloomy theology disturb my faith in its godlike powers and tendencies... I shut my eyes on none of its weaknesses and crimes. I understand the proofs by which disposition demonstrates that man is a wild beast... But injured, trampled on, and scorned as our nature is, I still turn to it with intense sympathy and strong hope.

We know much more about human nature, our origins and development, than we did in Channing's time. Science is on the exciting edge of learning much more about us, especially through the recent growth of brain research. Yet a contemporary theology of humanistic religious naturalism agrees with Channing's assessment of human beings. It is important, however, to be clear about the nature of both the grandeur and the misery of humankind.

The Nature of the Self

Humanistic naturalism maintains that human beings are part of nature and are rooted and grounded in the natural world. It rejects the Platonic-Cartesian dualism that holds that humans consist of a transient physical body allied with an eternal spiritual soul. What we call soul or spirit is simply a function of our brain and nervous systems, which are highly complex biological organs. What we call the self is the working together of our mental, physical, and emotional qualities. What we call thinking is simply a great deal of electricity flowing along membranes. Our emotions result from our neurotransmitters ejecting onto our brain cells.

As part of the natural world, humans have a kinship with other beings. The cells in our bodies are basically the same as those in other life-forms, although they are organized in different patterns. We are dependent on the resources of nature for our very survival and well-being, and we are made of the same stuff as the stars. Robert Weston's beautiful poetry still rings true:

> Out of the stars in their flight, out of the dust of eternity,
>   here have we come . . .
> Out of the stars have we come . . .
> Out of the sea to the land, up from darkness to light,
> Rising to walk and to fly, out of the sea trembled life . . .
> This is the marvel of life, rising to see and to know;
> Out of your heart, cry wonder: sing that we live.

Yet despite our kinship with all forms of life, humanistic religious naturalism maintains that each person is an absolutely unique individual, of great worth and inherently sacred. We have a great deal in common with other human beings—some of the same basic physical and emotional needs, the same basic instincts, and similar drives. Nevertheless, we are each unique and individual. The self is not something given to us at or before birth; it is shaped through a lifelong creative process of becoming. It is a complex mixture of instinctive tendencies and deliberative actions, of thinking, feeling, and willing.

A primary characteristic of the self is its capacity for growth; we can learn from our experiences and apply that learning to future experiences. Our growth consists of both continuity and change, in that we can build on what we have learned but also change ourselves—our attitudes, goals, and values. The ethical implication of evolution is growth and creativity. Learning and growth mean not only that we can learn new skills and acquire new knowledge but that we can grow in ways that enable us to become better, wiser, more loving, and more effective persons. This "gospel of growth" underlines the importance of education—not only formal education but also lifelong education in all its forms. As Bob Dylan says, "The person who is not busy growing is busy dying."

Humanistic religious naturalism encourages individuals to recognize and use their own creativity and power and to develop their own unique abilities. It holds that individuals should respect themselves as persons of dignity and value, knowing that only those who respect themselves can respect others, and it encourages them to fulfill their potential. It also acknowledges humankind's limitations. But, aware of the progress humanity has made in its many millennia of existence, it continues to have hope for the future and to believe in the human potential for good.

The Individual and the Community

In the modern Western world, the human self has been understood in terms of individual reason and self-consciousness. Along with liberalism in general, religious humanism has shared this notion, which leads to a highly individualistic conception of the self rather than a social understanding of what it means to be human. There are at least two problems with this conception. On the one hand, it is simply not correct. We are social selves and interdependent beings before we are individuals. On the other hand, our rampant individualism is destructive of both the individual, who needs connectedness to be fully human, and of society, which benefits from cooperation and a commitment to the public good.

In *Habits of the Heart*, sociologist Robert Bellah and his coauthors identify three types of individualism. *Biblical individualism* recognizes the needs of the individual but emphasizes each person's obligation to put the good of the group ahead of self-in-

terest. *Civic individualism* prioritizes the needs of the group, especially the city or the nation, and regards individualism as good
within the context of the larger common good. *Modern individualism* holds that the rights of the individual always take precedence
over a person's responsibility to the group. The authors maintain
that this third type characterizes today's American culture.

Many examples of modern individualism come to mind:
smokers who insist on their right to smoke inside offices where
others work; committee members who believe their right to get
their way trumps the will of the majority; corporation managers
who fire thousands of employees while their own multimillion-
dollar salaries are unaffected. In each of these examples, what is
perceived as the right of the individual takes precedence over the
individual's responsibility to others and to the common good.
Bellah doubts that a society characterized by modern individualism can endure. Cooperation, rather than cutthroat competition,
is necessary to sustain a political and economic community.

The thought of both John Dewey and G. H. Mead emphasizes
the social nature of the self. Whereas modernist philosophers had
seen the individual as primary and the society as a secondary collection of individuals, Dewey and Mead reversed this. They understood society to be a precondition for the existence of the
individual. The individual self is formed and shaped by the social
nexus into which it is born.

The human being is a social animal. We become individual
selves and develop those qualities that belong to our humanness
only in relationships—first in the family, then through associations
with larger groups. Martin Buber writes of the "dialogic life," for to
be human is to be in continuous dialogue with ourselves and others. Human beings grow in the context of their communities. We
are who and what we are largely because of the relationships that
have shaped us. We become human in and through a society. The
individual is dependent on the larger community in many ways.
Each time I buy groceries or clothing or gasoline, I know that I
stand at the end of a long process to which many people have contributed. We may feel as though we are separate and distinct indi-

viduals, and we may often act like separate and distinct individuals, but we are not. We are interdependent and interrelated.

Historically, Western religion has understood the individual as part of a larger community. In ancient times, the community was the tribe or the city-state, and the individual was less important than the community. In the Hebrew religion, Yahweh God made his covenant not with individuals but with the people of Israel, "You will be my people and I will be your God." The ancient Greeks did not see their own interests as different from that of the larger community. In some cultures today, the ethnic group or the nation, rather than the individual, is foremost.

As people who think and act for themselves and who value individual rights, humanists tend naturally to be highly individualistic. But humanistic religious naturalism also understands the individual as belonging to the universal human community and as having loyalties and responsibilities to that wider world. Humanistic naturalism must affirm the need for a deep sense of connection to the whole human community, a sense that my individual interest is less important than the interest of the society, that each of us is one cell in the body of seven billion cells. It is clear that in today's world, what happens almost anywhere affects everyone, either directly or indirectly. Such a realization reinforces a sense of the interdependence and unity of humankind.

The American emphasis on individual autonomy has grown considerably in the last several decades, as seen in the so-called "me generation." In his groundbreaking book, *Bowling Alone*, Robert Putnam documents a steady decline in American social and political participation in contrast to the greater involvement in civic affairs of earlier generations. Ours is a society in which the motto seems to be "Do your own thing." Bellah describes a "cancerous individualism" that produces a "culture of separation." He writes,

> In earlier days, the individualism in America was one that also honored community values. Today we have an ideology of individualism that simply encourages people to maximize personal advantage. This leads to a consumer politics in

which "What's in it for me" is all that matters, while considerations of the common good are increasingly irrelevant.

On scales developed by social scientists to measure the degree of individualism versus community commitment, the United States rates as the most individualistic nation in the world. Unfortunately, at the present time the ascendancy of conservative politics is only reinforcing individualism by its free market philosophy and its opposition to public support for programs that benefit society. The problem with this kind of autonomous individualism is that it teaches us to regard our own self-interest as more important than the common good.

Today's religious humanists need to reaffirm the value of human community, especially communities that work and act together for the common good. We need to proclaim that individualism and community are not opposites. Rather, they complement each other in that we become individual selves through relationships with others. The challenge is always to balance healthy individuality with a genuine sense of being part of a larger whole. This emphasis on community is one of the differences between religious and secular humanism. One of the roles of the humanistic religious community is to enable people to find a balance between their individuality and their commitment to the common good.

Human Freedom

Basic to humanistic religious naturalism is a conviction of the inherent worth of each human being and of the centrality of freedom—the power to will something and to carry it out. To be human is to be able to transcend ourselves, to stand outside ourselves to some degree and to stand above the situations in which we are involved. This self-transcendence is the basis of our freedom, but it is not absolute. Although we are not puppets in the control of other forces, our thoughts and actions are profoundly influenced by our genetic makeup, our social circumstances, and the way we are nurtured. Still, self-determination is possible, and we can enlarge its scope.

Freedom is the source of our uniqueness, and it is also the basis of both our creative and destructive powers. Though far from total, the power of choice lies at the core of our lives. Each of us must decide what we believe to be true and right, what criteria we should use in deciding this, and how we should live. Whatever role nature and nurture play in the decisions, barring neurological damage, each of us is ultimately responsible for our choices. Freedom is the essence of our humanness.

The evolutionary development of freedom, as depicted mythologically in the biblical story of humankind's expulsion from paradise, is instructive in that human history begins with an act of choice. In the story, the first humans live an animal-like existence in the Garden of Eden—without work, without freedom, and without thinking, but in complete harmony with nature. When they eat the forbidden fruit, they are depicted as disobeying God's command. Christianity sees this act of rebellion against authority as the beginning of sin and evil. However, it can also be seen as a mythological depiction of the beginning of human freedom. By asserting themselves and acting against God's command, Adam and Eve emerge from the prehuman stage of unconscious existence to the level of humanness and freedom. The story is a mythical depiction of an important aspect of human evolution. What in theology is called the "fall of man" should really be termed the ascent of humanity.

The story represents not only the reality of free choice but also the awareness of moral responsibility. The tree from which Adam and Eve eat represents the knowledge of good and evil. God says, "Behold, the man has become like one of us, knowing good and evil." To know good and evil and to have the freedom to choose one or the other is to be morally responsible for that choice. Freedom is the source of both humankind's grandeur and its misery.

Just as there is an innate desire for freedom, so also there is an instinctive human wish for submission. The responsibility that comes with freedom, the need to think and act for ourselves, is demanding. It is easier to submit to authority, as Dostoevsky so vividly told us in the famous "Legend of the Grand Inquisitor." In the time of the Spanish Inquisition, Jesus appears in Seville and restores a stricken child to life. The acclaim he receives is quickly hushed by the appearance of the old cardinal, the chief inquisitor. The inquisitor promptly jails Jesus, then tells him why he cannot allow him to remain in the city. "We have corrected your work and founded it on miracle, mystery and authority." He goes on to say that Jesus has made a fundamental mistake. Jesus wants people to be free, but they don't want freedom, the inquisitor says. They want security; they want to be told what to do and what to think. They want to be like sheep. "People are weaker and baser than you believed them to be," the Inquisitor says. "Respecting them less, you would have asked less of them."

Freedom requires the repudiation of external religious authority. Most religions rely on the teachings of sacred scriptures, the church, or certain religious leaders, such as Moses, Jesus, Buddha, or Mohammed. Humanistic religious naturalism insists instead that each person is his or her own authority in religious matters. We must rely not only on our individual experiences, our thoughts and affections, but also on those ideas and values we have learned from religious and secular traditions.

Freedom also means being able to think for ourselves in social, political, and economic matters. In an 1830 sermon called "Spiritual Freedom," William Ellery Channing famously proclaims,

> I call that mind free which jealously guards its intellectual rights and powers, which does not content itself with a passive or hereditary faith . . . . I call that mind free which is not passively framed by outward circumstances, and is not the creature of accidental impulse . . . . I call that mind free which protects itself against the usurpations of society, and which does not cower to human opinion.

As a humanistic religious naturalist, I want each person to be able to realize his or her own potential, freed from the crippling effects of poverty, malnutrition, and ignorance. These are the primary things that limit human freedom. The person who is poor, whose stomach is empty, and who has little education is far less free than the affluent, well-fed, well-educated individual. Both religious humanism and religious naturalism teach us to seek an end to poverty and malnutrition and to increase knowledge and understanding through education in order to expand individual freedom of choice, as well as to enhance the quality of human life.

In a previous chapter, I looked at the story of evolution as the primary story of religious naturalism. I suggest that the story of religious humanism is the story of the long struggle of the human race for freedom. It is the story of the struggle for political as well as religious freedom. It is the story of the struggle to abolish slavery in the ancient world—and in the modern world as well. It is the story of the Hebrew prophets who sought to change Judaism from a religion of laws and rituals to an ethical faith. It is the story of Jesus, who sought to make Judaism a religion of the heart instead of a religion of laws. It is the story of the Protestant Reformation, which sought to free religion from priestly and ecclesiastical authority, and the Second Vatican Council, which brought greater freedom to the Roman Catholic tradition. It is the story of the Buddha's reform of Hinduism and of liberalizing groups within Buddhism, such as Rissho Kosei-kai in Japan. It is the story of the early Unitarians in Europe and America, who insisted on freedom of belief and the use of reason in interpreting scriptures. It is the story of the Universalists, who freed people from a God of wrath and punishment and led them to a God of love. It is the story of all those who have sought to purge religion from authoritarianism and who have fought for greater political freedom over the ages. It is the story of the liberation of the mind from superstition and from religious dogmas that foster bigotry and hate. It is the story of the rise of democracy, freeing people from political authoritarianism. It is the story of the women and men who have worked for equal rights for people of color, and the story of those who fought and are fighting for equality for women and gay people. It is the story of all those who have worked to make human life more truly free and therefore more fully human.

Good and Evil

Religious humanism has been justly accused of failing to take seriously enough the depth of evil in humankind and thus of being too optimistic in its understanding of human nature. Some of this may reflect a reaction against traditional Christian doctrines of sin and the need for redemption. But at a deeper level, perhaps we humanists and religious liberals have not wanted to think about evil because we have been afraid to face it within ourselves. We have failed to acknowledge the demonic aspect of human nature. However, such a view is not inherent in religious humanism, and sin and evil can be understood within the context of humanistic religious naturalism. Without losing faith in human worth and dignity, religious humanists need to account for injustice, oppression, and exploitation—that is, for the demonic side of life. We need to acknowledge the magnitude of moral evil in the world and understand its sources: pride, egocentricity, and the desire for power over others.

For the purposes of this discussion, the word *good* refers to words or actions that foster the unfolding of the full powers of human life and serve the best interests of an individual or a community. Conversely, I use *evil* to mean words or actions that prevent or destroy the unfolding of the full powers of human life and are destructive of the well-being of an individual or a community.

The Christian tradition maintains that human beings have fallen from their original state of innocence into a condition of sinfulness. This is the famous doctrine of original sin, which holds that we are inherently depraved. Both liberal religion and the bulk of modern psychology maintain that human beings are born neither inherently good nor inherently evil. We are shaped by both our early upbringing and our genetic inheritance. Those infants and children who are loved and treated with caring and tenderness will, for the most part, become loving, caring, trusting adults.

On the other hand, the person brought up in circumstances characterized by distrust, violence, hostility, or abuse will be much more likely to exhibit those qualities. We have to qualify these statements, because we simply do not yet know enough about the role of our genetic inheritance in determining character. We know that some people have been able to transcend their violent upbringing and become productive adults. Many biologists and others believe that genetics plays a more important role than previously thought.

While there is much truth to the nurture thesis, it is not the whole story. We human beings were able to evolve over millions of years because of a strong instinct for survival—an instinct that remains with us in the form of egocentricity. It is "natural" for us to seek the best we can for ourselves. Yet this often leads to conflict with others who are also seeking what they believe is best for them. When this desire for the best for one's self is not balanced by empathy and concern for the needs of others, it can lead to destructive or evil behavior.

The Enron story is a case in point. The leaders of that corporation found many ways to enrich themselves through fraud and misrepresentation, eventually causing their employees to lose their jobs and their retirement savings, their investors to lose money, and many other people to pay excessive energy bills. One way of describing what happened is to say that the instinct for self-preservation of the corporate heads was transmuted into self-aggrandizement that was harmful to others. The dictator whose greed and lust for power deprives his people of the basic necessities of life is another example of the transmutation of self-preservation into evil. The company that pollutes the air and water with the toxic wastes of its manufacturing process is injuring both human and nonhuman life. Reinhold Niebuhr maintains that even our rationality and our wills are adversely affected by our egocentricity. He explains in *An Interpretation of Christian Ethics*,

No matter how much man's rationality is refined, he will always see the total situation in which he is involved from a limited perspective; he will never be able to divorce his reason from its organic relations with the natural impulse of survival with which nature has endowed him; and he will never be able to escape the sin of accentuating his natural will-to-live into an imperial will-to-power.

It is undeniable that self-interest lies at the very root of actions that result in harm or evil. Even those of us who have not committed egregiously harmful acts can point to times when we asserted our own self-interest in ways that were hurtful to others. In some cases we did not intend to hurt anyone, but at other times we did. Such is the power of egocentricity.

Further, human beings can perpetrate acts of extreme hatred and cruelty, sometimes without any conscious purpose. We can harm people we love and then regret it, and we can commit acts of violence that result in irreparable injuries. We have both a creative, constructive side and a demonic, destructive one. Life is filled with tragedy as well as with grandeur. Evil is a potential in every one of us.

The human tendency toward egocentricity takes a variety of forms. At the extreme, our innate self-centeredness can become what Erich Fromm called "malignant narcissism." This is narcissism so total that the person infected with it is completely devoid of empathy or any respect for others. The malignant narcissist is characterized by grandiosity, fantasies of unlimited power and success, and a need for excessive admiration. These are people so totally self-absorbed that it does not occur to them to think of the effects of their actions on others. Scott Peck writes, "The blindness of the narcissist to others can extend even beyond a lack of empathy; narcissists may not 'see' others at all."

Psychologist Alfred Adler suggests that each of us seeks recognition, seeks to be seen and understood as important. In his view, this need stems from the fact that as infants, we felt inferior to our adult caretakers, who could do so many things we could not—feed us, warm us when we were cold, transport us from one place to another, open doors, and so on. In our adult life, this need may take the form of seeking to be recognized as more powerful, more famous, or wealthier than others. This need to be superior in some way can lead to great accomplishments. But it can also lead us to cause and/or take pleasure in others' misfortune. Our natural will to live is transmuted into a will to power.

As Unitarian Universalist minister Richard Gilbert writes in *The Prophetic Imperative,*

> Human nature exists in a tension between the will to mutuality and the will to power. Our will is ambiguous. While we have the potential to transcend ourselves, we can also be utterly selfish. Our potential for creativity is matched by our propensity for destruction. . . . The line between good and evil runs right through the middle of each human heart.

No matter how well-meaning and well-intentioned each of us may try to be, no matter how hard we may try to do what fosters life and is beneficial to others, our freedom of choice means that each of us falls short many times and pursues actions that are harmful. We are all capable of evil acts as well as acts of kindness, love, and generosity.

Humanistic religious naturalism acknowledges the complex moral make-up of human nature and encourages us to live reflectively, aware of the consequences of our actions, and to live conscientiously and sensitively, maximizing our beneficial actions and minimizing our destructive ones.

Sin is not a popular concept among religious liberals, but properly understood it is very important. Sin means to engage in actions and attitudes that alienate a person from his or her true self and from others. Sin is thus a relational concept. It is that which interferes with or prevents authentic relationships. Three attitudes that are most often the source of destructive actions are pride, greed, and apathy.

Pride, or hubris, stems from having an overly high opinion of one's self. It results in haughty or arrogant behavior, which often involves putting another person down in order to build one's self up. Of course, such pride is very different from the justifiable pride a person can feel in a sense of accomplishment and worthiness. The pride we're talking about is the assertion of superiority and the expectation of obedience or agreement. It destroys the possibility of love and community because these are predicated on equality. Reinhold Niebuhr regards human beings as existing at the juncture of nature and spirit, between freedom and necessity. The fact that we are both free and limited creates anxiety, from which we try to escape by denying one dimension or the other. The attempt to deny our finitude leads to excessive pride; the attempt to deny our higher nature leads to a life of sensuality. Either causes a person to fail to become fully human.

Greed is an example of self-aggrandizement and a form of sensuality. It is the result of fear—fear of personal or financial insufficiency. Those who are greedy use possessions as a means of exalting themselves or proving that they are better, more important, or more powerful than others. Greed is dehumanizing, since a greedy person regards other people as objects to be exploited for his or her purposes rather than ends in themselves. Thus greed alienates the individual from his or her true self and from others.

Perhaps the best-known story about the harmful effects of greed is the Midas myth. When King Midas is granted one wish by the god Bacchus, he asks that everything he touches be turned into gold. His wish is granted, but he can not eat his food since it too turns into gold, and when he embraces his beloved daughter he turns her into gold as well. Greed destroys our humanity because it cuts off love and nourishment to the spirit.

Apathy or indifference stems from a self-centeredness so strong that it allows one to remain untouched by the suffering of others. Lacking in empathy, the apathetic person stands idly by while others are harmed, often using the excuse that he or she is powerless to help. In the late twentieth century, it was said that Americans had a bad case of "compassion fatigue." As a nation, we became indifferent to the plight of those who were less well off. That indifference seems to have increased in the twenty-first century, at least if public policies are any indication. The high percentage of Americans who fail to vote would seem to be another example of apathy. Failure to act because of indifference can result in evil, as it did on the part of those Germans in the 1930s who saw the evil in Nazism but did nothing to fight it.

Sin and evil can also take the form of idolatry, the elevation of something relative or partial to the status of what is ultimate or whole. That is the demythologized meaning of the biblical commandment to "have no other gods before me." Idolatry takes many forms. It is not just the worship of a golden calf or some other physical object. When a person regards his or her nation as the ultimate reality—the "my country, right or wrong" mentality—that is idolatry. Racism and ethnocentrism represent an idolatry of one's own racial or ethnic characteristics or culture. Religious idolatry occurs when one set of religious views and doctrines (and that includes humanistic religious naturalism) is regarded as the absolute truth. When pride and greed elevate the self into a god-like being, that is idolatry of the self. In all of these forms, idolatry relegates one group of people to inferior status, where they may become victims of prejudice and oppression.

Evil, in a particularly subtle and dangerous manifestation, can result from good that is distorted. The United States' involvement in Vietnam, for example, came from good intentions, but it resulted in hundreds of thousands of deaths and untold devastation. On a personal level, it is wise to take care of ourselves, but self-care can quickly become warped into self-absorption. Piety and virtue are positive traits, but they become harmful if they lead to self-righteousness and arrogance. Urban renewal may stem from good intentions, but those it displaces may be left homeless. Furthermore, evil can be the result of ignorance or a failure to think critically about the likely results of an action. If I am in a hurry and drive my car too fast, I may have an accident that injures or kills another person. Unintentional harm is still harm.

Evil is not only an individual matter. It is also something human societies are guilty of, usually resulting in greater harm than what individuals do. War is an obvious example. The impe-rialistic policies of Germany and Japan in the mid-twentieth cen-tury killed millions of innocent people and caused incredible destruction. Nations, like individuals, seek what they understand to be their own self-interest, and that often leads to harm for other nations. In his book *Moral Man and Immoral Society*, Reinhold Niebuhr shows that while individuals sometimes transcend their own self-interest, nations never do.

Policies that obscenely increase the wealth of the rich at the expense of the poor are another example of social evil. Recently we have seen tax policies that benefit the wealthiest few while jeopardizing the future fiscal health of the nation, as well as envi-ronmental policies that help corporations make more money but pollute the air and water, risking harm to human beings and other living things.

Liberal religion, including religious humanism, has too long held to a naive idea of sin and evil that fails to acknowledge the depth and pervasiveness of evil in humankind and the extent to which the human will is affected by egocentricity. As a result, liber-alism has taught that perpetual human progress is possible through love and the use of reason. Corliss Lamont, in *The Philosophy of Humanism*, expresses his belief "that human beings, using their own intelligence and cooperating liberally with one an-other, can build an enduring citadel of peace and beauty upon this earth." However, if reason and love are tainted by egocentricity, evil is not so easily eradicated and progress is not so certain or simple. It will be well if religious humanism retains its essentially opti-mistic view of human life, but that view must be balanced with a greater awareness of the destructive side and the tragic dimension of existence. This awareness is one of the gifts of naturalism.

Salvation

The humanist is primarily concerned with fulfilling the best and the highest potential that is in us in this life, not with what happens after death. Religious humanism must take seriously the fact that human self-centeredness and selfishness often lead to negative consequences that are rightly described as demonic or evil. But humanism must also affirm that this is not the whole story, that "salvation" is possible. Even though evil will never be eliminated—the egocentricity at its source is too much a part of our evolutionary heritage—it can be reduced in several ways.

The first is through education—providing more and better education in general, and training in child-rearing and ethics in particular. Raising general educational levels and increasing the quality of education from kindergarten through college can produce beneficial results. Better prenatal care and nutritional training for pregnant women is also important, as is teaching parents how to raise loving infants and children. Ethics education in high school and college, taught from a nonsectarian perspective, can enable people to learn what it means to live ethically and why living ethically is important.

Creating the social conditions for a more humane and caring society is another important way to reduce human destructiveness. The social nature of human life means that the health of the individual is closely tied to the health of the society. As twentieth-century Unitarian minister John Haynes Holmes puts it, "The church will care. . . not so much for emancipating men from what we call sin, as for emancipating them from the conditions of life and labor which make sin inevitable; not so much for saving souls as for saving the society which molds the soul for eternal good or ill." Raising the standard of living of low-income families through living wage legislation, universal medical insurance, and better public education would create better social conditions. The eradication of discrimination based on race, gender, and sexual orientation would also enable more people to live more productive lives.

One of our social ills is the failure to place a higher priority on the public good. The rampant individualism of American culture reinforces selfish behavior and the self-centered mindset.

Exaggerated self-interest and competition need to be replaced by an attitude of cooperation and human solidarity, the sense that the common good is more important than that of one individual. That would be a sea change in our attitudes and in the way society is organized, but it is an ideal to work for, with the hope that a few seeds planted now will eventually take root. John Dietrich described such a society when he urged, in a 1925 address, that we turn "away from society based on the motive of personal gain toward a society based on the idea of service to all; away from a society that is chiefly acquisitive toward a society that is pre-eminently cooperative; in which every individual and each group alike will be judged and respected and rewarded, not by the amount of material wealth they have been able to accumulate, but by the actual service they have rendered to the common good of humanity, of which each is an integral member."

Human Grandeur

Humanistic religious naturalism emphasizes the importance of each individual and the responsibility we each have for ourselves and for the world in which we live. Recognizing human limitations and the reality of sin and evil, we can still have faith and confidence in humankind as the only possible source of world progress. We will not build Lamont's "enduring citadel of peace and beauty upon this earth" in this or the next generation, but that should not deter us from wholehearted efforts in that direction. Progress is possible; it's just not as rapid or as complete as we would like, and there are always serious challenges and setbacks along the way.

Thus, despite the problem of self-centeredness and the terrible evil and destructiveness it often leads to, humanistic religious naturalism's assessment of human beings is more positive than negative. Our intelligence, our ability to think critically and constructively, our freedom and responsibility, our creativity, and our altruism are qualities that point to the grandeur of human beings. The great works of literature, art, architecture, and philosophy;

the truly incredible discoveries of modern physics, astronomy and biology; the remarkable life-saving and life-enhancing advances of modern medicine; the incomparable achievements in many other fields of endeavor that have enriched our lives—all these attest to the greatness of humankind. Add to these the countless people whose actions have contributed to human betterment but whose names are lost to history—people who in many cases made significant personal sacrifices for the greater good. At the end of her great novel *Middlemarch*, George Eliot offers this beautiful, and inspiring, description of her hero, Dorothea:

> Her full nature . . . spent itself in channels which had no great name on the earth. But the effect of her being on those around her was incalculably diffusive: for the growing good of the world is partly dependent on unhistoric acts, and that things are not so ill with you and me as they might have been is half owing to the number who lived faithfully a hidden life, and who rest in unvisited tombs.

The human race has done so many extraordinary things, and there is much that is good in us. Alexander Pope refers to the human being as "a being darkly wise and rudely great" and "the glory, jest, and riddle of the world." This is the great paradox of human existence: We have two sides, and it is important to take full account of both aspects of our humanness. But for each of us as individuals, it is even more important to serve what Lincoln called "the better angels of our nature."

Death

The traditional Western view of human nature is the dualistic Platonic and Cartesian notion that we consist of an immortal spiritual substance, the mind or soul, temporarily imprisoned in a physical body. In his papal encyclical *Donum Vitae*, Pope John Paul II reaffirms this view when he writes that the human body "cannot be considered as a mere complex of tissues, organs and functions," for it exists in "substantial union with a spiritual soul." In this perspective, the body dies but the immortal soul goes on to an afterlife.

A second Christian interpretation is that the body and soul are united, that both end with death and that God will resurrect the dead in some unknown form at the end of history. In this view, no part of the human being is immortal, and life after death is possible only because of the gracious act of God. This idea seems more in keeping with the Biblical understanding, for the Hebrews did not share the Greek notion of an immortal soul, and in the New Testament Paul writes of the resurrection of the "spiritual body." In the Garden of Eden story, death is seen as a punishment for sin. But humanist and naturalist perspectives regard death as merely nature's way of making room for others—to give others life on this beautiful earth and to enable parents to enjoy children and grandchildren. Cell biologist and religious naturalist Ursula Goodenough writes that from a biological standpoint, organisms could not be multicellular without death:

> Sex without death gets us single-celled algae and fungi; sex with a mortal soma gets you the rest of the eukaryotic crea- tures. Death is the price paid to have trees and clams and birds and grasshoppers, and death is the price paid to have human consciousness, to be aware of all that shimmering awareness and all that love. My somatic life is the wondrous gift wrought by my forthcoming death.

For the religious humanist death is not evil, but it is final.

In this era when it is possible to sustain life artificially for many years through medical technology, the question of when death occurs is not always a simple one. Humanistic religious nat- uralists will usually depend on the opinions of medical scientists to answer this question. Since modern science knows that the brain is what regulates, integrates, instructs, and unifies the entire human organism, a permanently nonfunctioning brain defines death, even though some bodily functions may be continued through life support technology. Neurologists have established criteria defining brain death, and no one who has met those criteria has survived.

Since humanistic naturalism asserts the unity of the body and the mind or soul, it does not consider any aspect of a human being to be immortal in the usual sense. When the body dies, all that we are—mind, soul, spirit—dies, for these are functions of a physical being. In the words of John Dietrich, "Man, like everything else, is a temporary expression of the forces of the universe, which momentarily rose to the plane of consciousness and then goes back into the state whence he came, having made his contribution, good or bad, to the boundless sweep of being."

We live on only in the memories of those who have loved us and the contributions we have made to the world. Like a star whose light is quenched but continues to be visible on earth, so our lives continue to shine after we have died. Humanistic religious naturalism affirms that we live on after death through what we have left behind, and that is yet another motivation for contributing as much as we can to human betterment.

Many humanists and naturalists also use their deaths to make their lives count more by donating their bodies to medical research or their organs to extend others' lives. With no life beyond to anticipate, we are free to emphasize making the most of this life—to live well, to know the love of friends and family, to experience the beauty and wonder of nature, to enjoy broadening one's knowledge and deepening one's understanding, and to play a role in making the world a better place. George Eliot expresses this thought beautifully in her familiar poem:

> Oh, may I join the choir invisible
> Of those immortal dead who live again
> In minds made better by their presence; live
> In pulses stirred to generosity,
> In deeds of daring rectitude, in scorn
> For miserable aims that end with self,

In thoughts sublime that pierce the night like stars,
And with their mild persistence urge men's search
To vaster issues. So to live is heaven:
To make undying music in the world.

The Responsible Search for Truth

OUR SOCIETY TODAY is engaged in a "culture war" that pervades politics as well as religion and that can be understood as a conflict between two modes of thought. One is grounded in revelation from a supernatural source as interpreted by evangelical preachers, Roman Catholic priests, and others. This kind of thinking sees the world in terms of absolute truth and absolute moral values. It is dualistic in that it thinks in terms of natural and supernatural, temporal and eternal, body and soul. Human beings are creatures of a supernatural God, and our task is to obey his will and fit our lives into his divine plan. It claims its truths to be final and absolute because it is based on a higher authority.

The other mode of thought, that which humanistic religious naturalism espouses, relies on the human ability to use our intelligence and our reasoning capacity to determine what is true and right. It relies on observation, reflection, critical thinking, and testing by experimentation, and it builds on what is learned in this way from generation to generation to expand knowledge and understanding. It holds that supernatural revelation is not reliable, nor are other direct, unmediated claims to truth. It does not claim absolute certainty, for it regards knowledge as dynamic and growing as humankind learns more about the world and human nature. Instead it maintains that our knowledge involves degrees of probability.

Using the terms *Skeptics and True Believers*, Chet Raymo describes the two perspectives well:

> Skeptics are children of the Scientific Revolution and the Enlightenment. They are always a little lost in the vastness of the cosmos, but they trust the ability of the human mind to make sense of the world. They accept the evolving nature of truth and are willing to live with a measure of uncertainty. Their world is colored in shades of gray. . . . Since they hold their truths tentatively, Skeptics are tolerant of cultural and religious diversity.
>
> True Believers are less confident that humans can sort things out for themselves. They look for help from outside— from God, spirits, or extraterrestrials. Their world is black and white. They seek simple and certain truths, provided by a source that is more reliable than the human mind. . . . They are repulsed by diversity, comforted by dogma, and respectful of authority.

The humanist's way of thinking, practiced by Raymo's Skeptics, involves questioning basic assumptions and convictions, including one's own. It demands evidence for its conclusions. It tends to be skeptical about all claims to knowledge and truth that have not been verified by empiricism or critical intelligence. It is aware of the human tendency to believe what we want to believe or what gives us security or comfort or joy, whether or not it can be shown to be true. It knows that we humans have almost unlimited powers of self-deception. Humanistic religious naturalism shares this understanding with traditional humanism and maintains that we should rely on empirical observation and critical thinking in arriving at what we believe. But humanistic naturalists also know that what we believe to be true must be corroborated by the observations and critical thinking of others, or else it may prove to be merely our own viewpoint.

Traditionally, this mode of thought has been called reason. But in this age of neo-romantic postmodernism, reason and critical thinking are out of favor and feelings are accepted as a source of truth. Postmodernists even assert that all efforts to ascertain what is true are invalid, because all are culturally conditioned. And they point out that reason has too often been used to justify political and economic policies that have been harmful to the common good. Both the Vietnam war and tax cuts for the wealthy were given rational justification despite the immense harm of the former and the latter's dramatic increase of the national debt. Human beings have used their intelligence and reasoning powers to confirm their prejudices and to exploit their fellow human beings. It seems that we are not only rational animals but also rationalizing animals. Moreover, humanism's emphasis on reason and the scientific method has led to the accusation that humanism is a cold, sterile, one-dimensional way of life that lacks warmth and caring. Humanists are somewhat justifiably accused of being all head and no heart.

Some of the criticisms of reason are based on a narrow understanding of what reason means, the view that reason refers to a coldly logical way of thinking. Rem Edwards suggests a larger understanding of reason: "Being reasonable involves more than thinking logically; it involves a comprehensiveness of vision and enlightenment, fairness and impartiality of judgment, and freedom from external and nonrational pressures." When humanistic religious naturalists refer to depending on reason, we should have this larger meaning in mind. This type of thinking has no place for dogmatism. The important thing is to be a reflective and reasonable person who does not accept beliefs as true simply because they are taught or because someone or some group believes them. On the other hand, no one can possibly verify everything, so we are all dependent on the results of the work of others. It then becomes important that we choose responsible experts or studies to depend on. The spherical shape of the earth, the rotation of the earth around the sun, the fact that some infections are caused by bacteria, the chemical composition of elements, biological evolution through the process of natural selection, the importance to our health of eating fruits and vegetables—these are but a few of the many possible examples of universally accepted knowledge that few of us feel the need to verify for ourselves.

The Scientific-Empirical Method

The form of rationality or intelligence that provides the most reliable knowledge about nature, including human nature, is the scientific-empirical method. We depend on the scientific method for everything from the benefits of medical and pharmaceutical research to knowledge about the care of plants, which foods are more nutritious, and many more modern advances.

Most of us use our intelligence and a simple form of the scientific-empirical method for solving various kinds of problems in daily life. The scientific-empirical method can be understood as simply a version of the process of experimentation or trial and error. John Dewey, in his book *How We Think*, suggests that the scientific method follows five basic steps. First we identify the problem; then we analyze and clarify the nature of the problem through observation and reflection. In the third step, we note possible solutions or working hypotheses. Step four involves reflecting on the various implications or consequences of each possible solution or hypothesis. And finally we verify the solution adopted.

My recent bout with pneumonia illustrates Dewey's five steps. My problem (step one) was a great deal of coughing and an abnormally high temperature. My physician listened to my breathing (step two) and made the diagnosis. We discussed several antibiotics (step three), some of which I rejected because of a previous allergic experience (step four). The antibiotic the doctor recommended cured my pneumonia (step five). Had it not, we would have had to go back through the last three or four steps again until I was cured, because this method includes both experience and experimentation. Something like that process occurs in varying degrees of sophistication in many of our efforts to determine what is true. To verify the outcome, we ask the pragmatic question, "Did it work?"

It is a mistake, however, to think that the scientific method always yields certainty; what it offers are degrees of probability. The limitations of being human make absolute certainty impossible in many cases. Our understanding of the world through the natural sciences changes somewhat as new discoveries are made and as new, more sophisticated equipment is developed for observing nature. Our understanding of human nature also changes through the discoveries of the human sciences. Therefore it is important to retain an open mind, but the fact that we are not privy to absolute truth does not mean that we have no reliable knowledge.

While the scientific-empirical method is the best method for discovering knowledge about the world, it is not enough in itself, for it can be used for heinous purposes. The actions of Nazi scientists illustrate the demonic uses to which science can be put. Knowledge must be used for humane and socially beneficial purposes. The application of scientific knowledge raises the question of values, which are matters of judgment and usually cannot be determined by observation, experiment, and empirical verification. Instead, our moral and religious views involve that part of ourselves we call the emotions.

The Role of the Emotions

In his groundbreaking book *Emotional Intelligence*, Daniel Goleman writes,

> A view of human nature that ignores the power of emotions is sadly shortsighted. . . . As we all know from experience, when it comes to shaping our decisions and our actions, feeling counts every bit as much—and often more—than thought. We have gone too far in emphasizing the value and import of the purely rational . . . in human life.

Goleman suggests that human beings have two fundamentally different ways of knowing. He calls them the rational mind and the emotional mind, and he notes that they correspond more or less to the popular distinction between head and heart. He also notes that there are gradations in the control the rational has over the emotional, so that "the more intense the feeling, the more dominant the emotional mind becomes—and the more ineffectual the rational. This is an arrangement that seems to stem from eons of evolutionary advantage to having emotions and intuitions guide our instantaneous response in situations where our lives are in peril—and where pausing to think over what to do could cost us our lives."

For the most part, the two minds operate in harmony. This balance between the emotional and rational minds is attained by a dialogue between the two, with each informing and refining the input of the other. For instance, because I am committed intellectually to the worth of every person, I am in favor of gay rights. I also feel strongly that gay people deserve all the rights and privileges that I and other straight people have. In this case, my emotions reinforce my rationality. On the other hand, sometimes the rational mind must veto the contribution of the emotions. I may be emotionally drawn to a particular automobile, but when I consider its price and the cost of operating it, I decide on a less costly and less emotionally appealing car. In this case, my rationality trumps my feelings.

Goleman cites neuroscientific research suggesting that feelings are actually indispensable for rational decisions because "they point us in the proper direction. . . . In the dance of feeling and thought the emotional faculty guides our moment-to-moment decisions, working hand-in-hand with the rational mind, enabling—or disabling—thought itself."

In an important book, *Upheavals of Thought: The Intelligence of Emotions*, University of Chicago scholar Martha Nussbaum expands on Goleman's thesis. She makes a convincing argument that emotions pervade the way we think and that they are part of what makes us human. In Nussbaum's view, it is not so much that we have two minds, a thinking mind and an emotional mind, as it is that our one mind consists of both rationality and affect. She sug-

gests that our emotions are suffused with intelligence and dis-
cernment and are therefore a source of deep awareness and understanding. Emotions, she maintains, are judgments of values.
We react with grief at the death of a loved one, for example, because we value that person highly. We become angry when
Congress passes legislation that promotes the interests of the big
oil companies because we recognize the injustice involved.
The role of the emotions is especially pronounced in making
ethical decisions. Antonio Damasio found that patients with a severely damaged prefrontal lobe of the brain—the location of the
brain's emotional centers—could not make moral decisions or decide among alternatives for future action. Otherwise their reasoning was not impaired. Damasio concluded that "feeling was an
integral component of the machinery of reason."

It is probably true that in most responsible truth-seeking and
decision-making, we rely on both head and heart, intelligence and
affect. The two engage in a reciprocity, a kind of dialogue, when
we are arriving at a decision—whether it is a decision about what
stereo system to buy or what position to take on issues such as
abortion, euthanasia, or sex education. Sometimes our head and
heart agree, and sometimes they disagree, with one or the other
winning. I trace my motivation for social action to my feelings of
compassion and empathy for poor and oppressed people, but
those emotions are built on a foundation of respect for all people.
What I do in response to those feelings is informed and shaped by
my intelligence, by what I can learn about the needs of poor people and the strategies that work best in addressing those needs.

John Dewey maintained that "there is no opposition" between
intelligence and emotion and that "there is such a thing as passionate intelligence." Humanistic religious naturalism needs to affirm the role of feelings like compassion and empathy in our
search for what is true and in our decision-making process, while
continuing to affirm the importance of reason and intelligence.

Testing Religious and Moral Views

By applying the pragmatic test to religious beliefs and moral perspectives, we can verify their truth or determine their falsehood. The test for religious and moral views is both whether they work and how they work. One test of a religious belief is, of course, whether it squares with what we know about the world. But another test is its effect on the individual who holds it. Does it enable that person to be a happier, more productive, more loving person whose life benefits others? Or does it produce an angry, self-centered, and authoritarian personality whose life is destructive to others? Another test is the effect of one's religious perspective on society. Does it benefit or harm the community? Does it lead to a society that is more just and more equitable or one that is unjust and unfair to some of its members? As Jesus said, "By their fruits you shall know them."

Finding a Balance

Traditional humanism emphasizes the importance of intelligence and the use of reason and critical thinking in determining what is true or valid. However, including the role played by the emotions adds a deeper dimension to our thinking processes. We think as whole persons, persons of both intelligence and feelings. Thinking often involves a dialogue between head and heart. Michael Werner suggests that "the human mind must be seen more as a 'committee of the minds,' with rational, emotional, instinctual, behavioral, etc., minds competing and interacting." Thinking and feeling are not two distinctly separate functions but rather feelings and emotions are continuous with thought and ideas. The dualism which assumes a bifurcation between emotions and thinking is erroneous.

Although feelings and intelligence work together, sometimes intelligence has to trump feelings. For example, some emotions lead to destructive behavior unless checked by intelligence. Anger at another person may cause me to want to harm that person, at which point my intelligence must rein in that emotion. On the other hand, compassion may lead a person to work to alleviate homelessness. That person's intelligence must then be used to determine what kind of work would be most effective and within her ability.

On another level, feeling that God exists and hears my prayers does not make it so, any more than feeling that ghosts inhabit my house makes that a reality. In these cases, critical reflection and a scientific-empirical mindset refute the idea that feeling something is real makes it real. Brain researchers have found evidence that the brain always wants to believe what makes a person happiest and most content. That is why we need to check such feelings with reality. And always our emotions need to be educated so they are in accord with our intelligence.

Our best source of truth about the world is through the use of our critical intelligence, but with respect to moral and religious questions we also use our emotional intelligence. After affirming the priority of the scientific method, the 1973 Humanist Manifesto II adds, "Reason should be balanced with compassion and empathy and the whole person fulfilled. Thus, we are not advocating the use of scientific intelligence independent of or in opposition to emotion, for we believe in the cultivation of feeling and love."

Using our knowledge well requires us to have a balance and a reciprocity between intelligence and emotions. Intelligence can serve to rein in or redirect emotions that are potentially destructive, and it can support socially beneficial emotions and direct them in effective ways. Emotions can inspire and motivate us in positive directions. In the words of Bertrand Russell, "The good life is one inspired by love and guided by knowledge."

Growing a Soul

A FEW YEARS AGO, as I was preparing a sermon, I asked some of the members of my congregation what they understood by the word *spirituality*. I got a number of different answers. Some said things like, "I'm looking for something more to my life, something deeper and more satisfying. I'm not sure exactly what it is I'm looking for, but that's what I call spirituality." Others said they were seeking a deeper meaning and purpose than they had found thus far. Some said they were looking for something to replace the faith in God they had lost.

Spirituality was not easy for them to define, but it was clear that people were not entirely satisfied with their lives. They felt something was missing. Many were unable to see their lives in the context of a divine plan, and they were feeling an emptiness in their lives, a lack of meaning and purpose. It was not enough to go to work five days a week, watch television, go to movies, do some reading, attend a party here and there, and spend time with family. Without something deeper, these things were not enough.

For these people and for many others, the old myths, stories, symbols, and beliefs—the ideas that, through traditional religion, informed Western culture for two millennia—have lost their power and credibility. Once, they informed our thinking and satisfied our yearning to find something bigger than our own egos, something deeper and more meaningful than achieving and accumulating or having a good time. Now, for many, these myths and symbols no longer provide a context for meaning or a belief system.

However, the secular myth of salvation by science, technology, and economic growth has also proven to be shallow and insufficient. It cannot provide an adequate meaning and purpose to sustain our lives either. We live between the times: The old myths have died, but no new myth has yet arisen.

What has arisen instead is renewed interest in spirituality and the need for spiritual growth, despite the difficulty in articulating precisely what these terms mean. For some, *spirituality* implies supernaturalism, but that is far from the only interpretation possible. As a religious humanist, I use the word *spirituality* to refer to a quality of life in the here and now, a quality that has to do with genuineness, depth, and devotion to values other than my own self-interest.

Many humanists have been slow to accept the concept of spirituality, perhaps because they associate it with a supernatural dimension or with spiritualism. The older humanism, with its emphasis on reason and scientific method, has resisted anything that smacks of nonmaterial substance or seems to dilute rationality in religion. But the new humanism that has been emerging in the last twenty or so years has a place for spirituality, as long as it is understood in a this-worldly, naturalistic, and nontheistic sense.

Many people think of spirituality as an otherworldly pursuit —something requiring a cloistered life or a means of escaping the world, as if this life is something to get beyond. In his book *Reaching Out*, the late Roman Catholic priest Henri Nouwen tells of a priest who cancels his subscription to *The New York Times* because he finds that the news of wars and crimes distracts him from prayer and meditation. Nouwen comments,

> That is a sad story because it suggests that only by denying
> the world can you live in it, that only by surrounding your-
> self by an artificial, self-induced quietude can you live a spir-
> itual life. A real spiritual life does exactly the opposite: it

makes us so alert and aware of the world around us, that all that is and happens becomes part of our contemplation and meditation and invites us to a free and fearless response.

True spirituality does not mean that we are to turn our backs on the world, enter the cloister, and spend all our time in prayer and meditation. True spirituality is a quality of life in this world, a foundation and a center for our lives from which we can then live more meaningfully and minister more effectively to those around us.

Sharon Welch writes of her parents that they brought two criteria to their spirituality: "Do these spiritual practices and experiences makes us more loving?" and "Do these experiences change how we live?" She goes on to affirm her own nontheistic spirituality using these criteria and adds, "Spirituality was that which brought us into full engagement with the world around us."

My dictionary defines *spirit* as the animating or vital principle in humans—that which gives life to the physical organism in contrast to its purely material elements. In that sense, *spirit* is the breath of life. In fact, the word spirit is derived from the Latin *spiritus*, meaning breath. We can say that spirituality is that which makes life vital and worth living, that which gives us something to live for, that which deepens and broadens our lives, that which makes us truly human.

I want to suggest several meanings of spirituality that make sense to me as a humanistic religious naturalist. It would be a mistake to think that the meaning of spirituality must be encompassed by one definition, for spirituality means different things to different people. The meanings are not mutually exclusive, and in fact all can be understood as part of this broad concept.

The Depth Dimension

At the most basic level, spirituality refers to a quality of life that so often evades us when we are absorbed with work and family. I believe that the cry for spirituality is a cry for something deeper, more meaningful, and more lasting than the dehumanized world most people inhabit. Ours is a consumer society in which our psyches are bombarded with images of the things we are told we ought to own or do, and we push ourselves to work harder in order to afford them. The result is that between working, consuming, and taking care of what we own, we have little time for reflecting or relating to others at a level other than the superficial.

We are experiencing a profound crisis in values. People have discovered the emptiness of a life devoted to materialistic and hedonistic values, and they want to find values that are more meaningful and more enduring. Capitalism may be the best kind of economy, but when it becomes the kind of rampant consumer capitalism we have today in America, its effect on the human spirit is utterly dehumanizing and alienating. Everything, including one's self and other people, is seen and treated as a commodity. Television commercials attempt to manipulate us to buy certain products. Corporations "downsize" their workforces without any concern about workers losing their livelihoods. People are treated as commodities, as means to someone else's goal rather than as ends in themselves.

For centuries, people have looked to theistic religion for meaning and purpose in their lives, but humanistic religious naturalism can also play this role. To be fully human means to become more spiritual in this sense of seeking and finding a deeper meaning and purpose in life. At least part of that meaning and purpose can be found by emphasizing personal rather than material values. By affirming the primacy of such humanistic values as love and social, economic, and racial justice, humanistic religious naturalism provides the foundation for this deeper meaning.

I think of a woman who came to my congregation in the 1980s seeking a spiritual dimension to her life. She became involved in our choir, participated in adult education classes, and began tutoring African American young people in Washington, D.C. As a result of these activities, she felt that her life had a far greater sense of meaning and purpose. She had found what she had been looking for.

At the very least, spirituality involves forging deeper connections with others, with one's inner life, and with nature. Most of us live too much of our lives at a shallow and superficial level. We seek relationships that are more profound and more meaningful. In Unitarian Universalist and other churches, covenant groups or other long-term small groups have served this purpose for many, as have teaching in religious education programs, singing in the choir, serving on committees, and working with others for social justice.

Beauty

A second meaning of the word *spiritual* involves a suspension of ordinary experience and a transcendence of the self. For me, this is often associated with aesthetic or imaginative experience. Artistic creations such as painting, music, poetry, and literature are spiritual creations. They spring from the deep resources of life, and they evoke in us higher, nobler thoughts and feelings. They transport us out of the mundane world. Their beauty may also lead us to care less about material things and see our lives in a larger perspective. For humanistic religious naturalists, the arts can play an important role in spiritual renewal and growth as they can and do for others. Great works of art nourish our spirits, and through them we gain deeper insight into life and its meaning. Paul Tillich said in an address at New York's Museum of Art,

> The artist brings to our senses and through them to our whole being something of the depth of our world and of ourselves, something of the mystery of being. When we are grasped by a work of art things appear to us which were unknown before—possibilities of being, unthought-of powers, hidden in the depth of life which take hold of us.

Some time ago, viewing an exhibit of the paintings of the Dutch artist Vermeer gave me a feeling of serenity and peacefulness and a deep sense of the goodness of life.

Great music in particular feeds my soul. Life brings disappointments, sorrow, and pain; we suffer and die. Life is tragic. But the great symphonies of Beethoven, Brahms, and Dvorak do not leave us there. They proclaim that despite its sadness and pathos, life is good and joyful and worth living, and that humankind's grandeur is greater than its misery. I find that if I listen to great music, I cannot remain dispirited for long. Great music breathes new life into my soul. In the Hebrew scriptures, King Saul's insanity is cured overnight by the power of David's harp.

For centuries, philosophers have summarized the great values of life in three words: *beauty*, *truth*, and *goodness*. Much of religion has been concerned with the latter two to the neglect of beauty, but beauty feeds and nourishes the soul. Beauty is a source of both great pleasure and inspiration. Things of beauty also have the power to bring out the best in us, to evoke in us the desire to make our *lives* beautiful. Perhaps one way they do this is by freeing us from the narrow self-preoccupation that often afflicts us, enabling us to feel some of the same emotions the artist felt when he or she composed that music or painted that picture. James Dickey once said that "the themes of poetry are the possibility of love and the inevitability of death." Those are the themes of religion as well. Wrestling with them through the works of poets, playwrights, and novelists fosters the growth of the soul. In our desacralized world, artistic experience can provide the spiritual dimension that traditional religions once did.

Peak Experiences

In a fine book on secular humanism, *Humanism: Beliefs and Practices*, British scholar Jeaneane Fowler suggests that the word *spirituality* contains too much of the baggage of traditional religion for humanists. She therefore suggests that we need a different word to describe what she understands to be the essence of spiritual experience. *Spiritual experience*, as Fowler understands it, refers to those times "when the material world slips into insignificance for a moment or two, and the self experiences something of the depth of life, the *quality* of experience." It involves a suspension of ordinary perception and language, and it is usually stimulated by experiences such as an aesthetic awareness of beauty, the care of others, or a sense of awe and wonder at nature. These are moments when our egos are transcended. We experience a heightened awareness, a sense of unity and absorption in the object or activity, and we lose our usual sense of time and space. She then suggests that these are the very characteristics that humanistic psychologist Abraham Maslow described in what he called "peak experiences." Fowler recommends that humanists use this phrase instead of the word *spirituality*.

I have two problems with her suggestion. For one thing, I think spirituality is more than peak experiences. Although that is certainly one part of what is meant by spirituality, I do not limit it to the experience of self-transcendence. For another, I think it is important for humanists to give our own meaning to words like *spirituality*, which I believe is a concept with many layers of meaning.

Love of the Universe

One of my former students said that to her, the word *spirituality* refers to "love of the universe." As one who is filled with awe when I contemplate the beauty of the earth and the unimaginable vastness of the cosmos, I like that suggestion. To marvel at the beauty of a flower garden, the towering grandeur of an ancient oak tree, the majesty of mountain peaks, the remarkable instinctual behavior of birds and animals, the diversity of biological life—the literally millions of organisms from the submicroscopic to the mammoth—is part of what love of the universe entails. Oxford University zoologist Richard Dawkins agrees, as he affirms the spiritual dimension of science in words that ring true to a humanistic religious naturalist:

> All the great religions have a place for awe, for ecstatic transport at the wonder and beauty of creation. And it's exactly this feeling of spine-shivering, breath-catching awe—almost

worship—this flooding of the chest with ecstatic wonder, that modern science can provide. And it does so beyond the wildest dreams of saints and mystics. The fact that the supernatural has no place in our explanations, in our understanding of so much about the universe and life, doesn't diminish the awe. Quite the contrary. The merest glance through a microscope at the brain of an ant or through a telescope at a long-ago galaxy of a billion worlds is enough to render poky and parochial the very psalms of praise.

Within the notion of love of the universe I would include love of life and gratitude for one's time on this earth. Gratitude drives away feelings of resentment and despair and transforms us into generous and large-souled persons. As Carl Sagan proclaims, "When we recognize our place in an immensity of light-years and in the passage of ages, when we grasp the intricacy, beauty, and subtlety of life, then that soaring feeling, that sense of elation and humility combined, is surely spiritual."

Connectedness

My favorite definition of *spirituality* is Parker Palmer's: "Spirituality is the eternal human longing to be connected to something larger than one's own ego," to which I add, "something that enriches one's life and gives it meaning." For theists, the desire to connect to something larger than themselves means a yearning for God. For the humanistic religious naturalist, however, many things can give the kind of meaning and direction to our lives that the theist finds in a commitment to God. Humankind itself may be that transcendent object of our devotion—for humanism is committed to human betterment in any and every possible way—or it may be a particular community, such as one's family, religious community, or nation. One can also be committed to a cause, such as a specific social justice program. In the humanist and naturalist traditions, a kind of mystical feeling of being at one with all things may be the ultimate source of meaning and reverence.

The experience of countless people has been that their lives were made worthwhile by their commitment to and involvement in causes that contribute to human welfare and world betterment. I know from my own experience that what I have done for others and the efforts I have made to increase social justice have given a spiritual meaning and depth to my life it would not have had otherwise.

In many Unitarian Universalist churches today, there are two groups of people, those who emphasize spirituality and those who emphasize social justice. Often the people interested in spirituality do not have anything to do with social justice work, and the social justice workers do not care about spirituality. That is unfortunate, because rather than being two disparate ways of being religious, they belong together, two sides of one coin. Genuine spirituality should lead to social concern and engender a commitment to social justice, whereas social justice ministry without spirituality will lead to frustration and burnout. Many people have told me that doing social justice work was their spiritual practice and the source of their spiritual growth.

Jung writes that during the first half of life, we focus on gaining competence and mastery in a vocational field or raising children. But the second half of life must center on the soul—developing one's personal and spiritual life. If we do not do that, Jung believed, we will not achieve a sense of fulfillment and completeness when we face death.

A. Powell Davies, the great twentieth-century Unitarian minister, said that "life is just a chance to grow a soul." That is to say, life is a spiritual journey, and we are always on it whether we recognize it or not. Spirituality is not a new concept. It is an old word with new meanings for today, meanings that humanists as well as others can value. It is the result of living in deeper, more meaningful, and more loving ways and with devotion to causes greater than one's self.

Can We Be Good Without God?

THE IDEA THAT ethical living depends on belief in God and follow-ing his commands permeates our society. For this reason, there is a popular misconception that humanism is unethical, having no basis for differentiating between right and wrong. However, noth-ing could be farther from the truth.

The field of ethics includes both reflection about the basis and nature of ethics and the application of ethical principles to specific issues. The former is called *meta-ethics*, and the latter may be termed either *practical ethics* or *morality*. This chapter deals with meta-ethical discussions of whether or not religion is the basis of morality, the origin of ethics, the objectivity of ethics, and the pos-sibility of altruism.

We can use simple logic to show that religion is not the founda-tion of morality. To do this we must ask: Is something good because God wills it, or is it good independently of God's will? In *Euthyphro*, Plato asks the same question in these terms: "Is what is holy holy because the gods approve it, or do they approve it because it is holy?" The first view, that God determines or decides what is good, makes divine approval arbitrary. It means that if God were to determine that torture is "good," then torture would be a moral act. That is obviously unacceptable. Alternatively, if something must be good in order for God to approve it, then it is good independently of

God's approval, and therefore it is not God's approval that makes it good. For it is only if we have some prior knowledge of good that we can recognize something God wills as good.

We humans bring to bear our previously formed moral values. We recognize "God's laws" as good only because we already have a concept of what is good. What is good is independent of God or God's will, and ethics does not need to be grounded in a divine lawgiver. Thus, far from morality being based on religion, the ethical dimension of religion is derived from a prior morality. Since our concept of what is good is independent of God, the theist too must use his or her moral understanding to decide whether God's commands are good and hence to decide whether God is indeed God. This is an example of William R. Jones's notion of "functional ultimacy," illustrated by the Abraham and Isaac story, as discussed in the chapter "Changes and Challenges."

There is also an empirical way of demonstrating that theistic religion is not necessary to moral living. Based on a comprehensive survey, psychologist of religion David Wulff shows a consistent correlation between religious affiliation and "ethnocentrism, authoritarianism, dogmatism, social distance, rigidity, intolerance of ambiguity, and specific forms of prejudice, especially against Jews and blacks." It seems that religion is often identified with what many of us consider immoral attitudes and behavior. That religion does not necessarily lead to moral behavior can also be seen in Nazism, which, far from being an atheistic regime as is often assumed, claimed to be doing God's work by annihilating the Jews. And I would argue that many of the moral principles preached and practiced in evangelical Christian circles today are immoral at the societal level. In a recent article, Christian scholar Bill McKibben is equally critical of the Christian right's moral values. He writes, "It's hard to imagine a con much more audacious than making Christ the front man for tax cuts for the rich or the war in Iraq."

On the other hand, I think of many humanist members of my former congregation whose lives increased the moral wealth of humankind. I also think of well-known humanists who have contributed significantly to human betterment. These include Helen Caldicott, Frederick Douglass, Barbara Ehrenreich, Betty Friedan, John Kenneth Galbraith, Stephen Jay Gould, Abraham Maslow, Linus Pauling, A. Philip Randolph, Carl Rogers, Carl Sagan, Alice Walker, and Faye Wattleton. History is filled with highly moral people, both theists and nontheists. Sadly the opposite is true as well.

If morality is not grounded in a divinity, what then is the source or foundation of ethics and moral values?

The Origin of Morality

Are ethical principles and laws, such as love, justice, and human rights, given to humankind from a transcendent source, or do human beings create them? Philosophers and theologians have debated this question for centuries. The Western religious traditions, of course, maintain that a supernatural deity is the source of ethical laws. Religious humanism, however, affirms that ethical and moral principles are created by human beings, not derived from a source outside humankind.

The process of moral evolution began in our animal background. Scientists have identified numerous premoral feelings and behaviors in our evolutionary ancestors—hominid, primate, and mammalian. Apes, monkeys, dolphins, and whales exhibit behaviors that include cooperation, mutual aid, altruism, sympathy, peacemaking, and community concern. Chimpanzees, for example, have been observed to share food, thus exhibiting cooperation and altruism. After a conflict, chimps not involved in the conflict will touch, hug, and groom the combatants, especially the one who is most upset. Dolphins have been seen pushing sick or wounded members of a pod to the surface so they can catch their breath. Whales will defend a wounded whale by circling it and striking the water with their flukes in order to ward off fishing boats.

These premoral feelings and behaviors became part of the evolutionary heritage of humans. Moral sentiments evolved out of them through something like the following process: As humans began to live together in societies, it became apparent that unless each person's life was protected, no one would be safe. Thus the basic human instinct for self-preservation gave rise to the prohibition against murder. Without this basic moral restriction, conflicts of interest that were bound to arise would lead to loss of life. At first, the prohibition against murder applied only to one's family, tribe, or clan. As understanding grew, and as mutual interests and interdependence became clearer, this basic prohibition against taking life expanded to include progressively larger groups—clusters of tribes, nations. Finally, at its highest point of development, it evolved into the principle of respect for all human life.

In the same way, it is easy to see how the need for trust and reliability in relationships led to such moral values as the prohibition against stealing and the importance of telling the truth and keeping promises. Through thousands of generations, these moral precepts have been expanded and modified to include other moral values. Charles Darwin puts it this way: "Any animal whatever, endowed with well-marked social instincts, the parental and filial affections being here included, would inevitably acquire a moral sense or conscience, as soon as its intellectual powers had become as well, or nearly as well developed, as in man."

As humans began to cluster together in larger groups, it became necessary to codify morality in order to achieve social control. Religion was the institution that did that.

Edward O. Wilson, a Harvard University biologist, suggests that humans are "predisposed biologically to make certain choices. Through cultural evolution some of the choices are hardened into precepts, then into laws, and, if the predisposition or coercion is strong enough, into a belief in the command of God or the natural order of the universe." He adds that such human propensities as cooperativeness and empathy may be heritable, that "cooperative individuals generally survive longer and leave more offspring." As a result, "in the course of evolutionary history genes predisposing people toward cooperative behavior would have come to predominate in the human population as a whole."

In his 1993 book, *The Moral Sense*, political scientist James Q. Wilson makes a strong case for an innate human moral sense that includes certain universal, guiding moral instincts. His research found that all societies believe that murder and incest, lying, and breaking promises are wrong and that family loyalty and caring for children are morally important. Anthropologists have identified a number of moral traits valued in all cultures, traits they term "universals" and for which they have found no exceptions. Among these are affection, attachment, empathy, pride, shame, and generosity. The fact of their universality is further evidence of morality's evolutionary heritage.

Versions of the Golden Rule arose in several ancient cultures, including those in which theism was either weak or absent. Confucius proclaimed around 400 BCE, "What you do not want others to do to you, do not do to others." Around 375 BCE the Greek Isocrates said, "Do not do to others what would anger you if done to you by others." The Hindu Mahabharata (ca. 150 BCE) and the Stoic Epictetus (ca. 100 CE) also taught versions of the Golden Rule.

Clearly moral principles did not just drop down from heaven or miraculously appear on a large piece of stone, as in Cecil B. DeMille's movie *The Ten Commandments*. They gradually developed from the human experience of living in societies, and they have both a biological and a social basis. That moral principles have evolved over many centuries is evident to anyone who has studied history or anthropology or has read the Hebrew Bible (the Old Testament), in which the later writings demonstrate a higher level of moral understanding than the earlier ones. Jesus' teaching that we should love our enemies—which many biblical scholars consider his only original contribution to ethics—is an example of a moral value (love) being extended beyond one's own tribe, nation, or ethnic group to all of humankind. And of course, the history of the United States in the last two hundred years shows the change from a defense of human slavery as morally right to a recognition of the terrible evil that it is. The studies of Lawrence Kohlberg, encapsulated in his six stages of moral development, provide another example of this principle, applicable both to individuals and to humanity as a whole.

Moral thinking requires the ability to transcend ourselves, to put ourselves in the place of others and to ask how we would feel if we were in their situation. This capacity for empathy and self-transcendence, so essential to the moral process, develops gradually in children, as it must also have done in the history of the human race. Each of us has our personal perspective, reflecting our own interests. But through our rational and empathetic capacities, we realize that others also have their own personal interests. Our capacity to be reasonable enables us to distance ourselves from our own point of view and see things from a larger perspective. That ability is critical to ethical thinking.

This process of learning to see ourselves from the perspective of others is documented by Piaget's studies of moral development. Reuben Osborn, drawing on Piaget's work, writes,

> Moral consciousness grows . . . as the individual leaves behind the egocentric stage of psychological development. He becomes aware of others, not just as objects who can satisfy his needs, but as individuals sharing human life with him, its difficulties and perplexities, its promises and hopes. This sense of shared humanity lies at the base of morality. Without some degree of it no kind of society would be possible. That this is where goodness lies shows itself . . . in all the great religions which stress the brotherhood of man.

Applying empathy and self-transcendence to basic needs, it is possible to see how early feelings of fairness and caring evolved. People recognized that others needed to eat and to be sheltered and clothed, just as they did.

The moral process involves a combination of human needs, human experience, and reflecting about experience. As Basil Mitchell writes in *Morality: Religious and Secular,*

> Human life is such that people have needs which can be met and purposes which can be realized only if they recognize

obligations to help one another and to refrain from harming one another in certain specifiable ways. . . . Thus morality is not arbitrary, but is rooted in the social nature of man.

The fact that fundamental moral norms are derived from experience and empirically grounded gives them a high degree of validity.

Since one individual's needs and interests often conflict with those of another, it is the task of ethical reflection to formulate principles or guidelines that assist in deciding between conflicting interests. And it is the task of the individuals and groups within a society to develop their moral thinking and moral emotions to the point at which they act not solely out of self-interest but out of the interest of the whole.

Moral and ethical principles and values are of course passed on from one generation to another. Each generation can draw on the moral traditions of its culture, which represent a depository of ethical insight and practice based on human experience over long periods of time. Each person or generation does not have to create its moral principles *de novo*. But at the same time, inherited values must be subjected to critical and analytical thinking, not simply accepted secondhand. Ultimately, each of us must decide for ourselves what principles and values we accept, what we reject, and what we revise or reinterpret.

How morality is transmitted from generation to generation may be more complex than we have heretofore realized. Obviously, social mores and ethical principles are embedded in the culture and communicated from parent to child. It is also likely that certain moral feelings are encoded in our genes. If empathy is a genetic inheritance, as E. O. Wilson suggests, that would mean our ability to feel another's pain is inherent as well as learned, and that empathetic feelings are the basis of much of our moral capacity. The revulsion we feel when seeing pictures of the carnage caused by terrorist attacks, or of prisoners being tortured, has deep emotional roots.

Since moral values have evolved throughout human history, we can assume that they will continue to evolve. Ethical theory must allow not only for past development but also for the continued evolution of values, or at least for changes in the way those values are understood and applied.

There is much moral wisdom to be mined in the Judeo-Christian tradition, and it is important for the humanistic religious naturalist to draw on that wisdom. If it does not have the authority of divinity, it can have the authority of the experience of morally sensitive persons. The same can be said for other religious and secular traditions. In the words of John Ruskin Clark from *The Great Living System*:

> Norms of good and evil, of right and wrong, did not spring full-blown from somebody's head; they developed slowly over generations of trial and error. It is part of the mark of being human that we benefit from the experience of others. . . . To recognize that concepts of good and evil are derived from human experience is to give them a timeless validity. . . . The realization that morals are empirically grounded does not invalidate traditional norms, it greatly reinforces them.

Moral Relativism

The fact that it is grounded in human experience rather than divine authority has led critics to contend that a humanist ethic has no certain foundation, and that it is "relative" to the culture or to the whim of each individual as opposed to being absolutely true for all people in all cultures. This leads to the view that relativism means "anything goes" and that there are, in effect, no moral values or principles. Critics of humanist ethics usually come from an authoritarian religious position, one that claims its ethical principles come from a supernatural God and therefore are absolutely certain and applicable at all times and in all circumstances. However, since humanist ethics arise out of human experience and reflection, they have as firm a foundation as it is possible for anything human to have.

Moreover, humanist ethics are objective, not subjective, because they are independent of the individual. Our moral sentiments and behaviors evolved over hundreds of thousands of years. The basic principles were created not by us but by many generations of our ancestors. In his book *The Science of Good and Evil*, Michael Shermer writes,

> Morality exists outside the human mind in the sense of being not just a trait of individual humans, but a human trait, that is, a human universal. . . . We simply inherit [moral sentiments and behaviors], fine-tune and tweak them according to our cultural preferences, and apply them within our unique historical circumstances. In this sense, moral sentiments and behaviors exist beyond us, as products of an impersonal force called evolution. In the same way evolution transcends culture, morality and ethics transcend culture, because the latter are direct products of the former. Given this presupposition it seems reasonable to be both a transcendentalist and an empiricist, or what I call a transcendent empiricist. Transcendent empiricism avoids supernaturalism as an explanation of morality, and yet grounds morality on something other than the pure relativism of culturally determined ethics.

We human beings are limited to what we can know and experience. To criticize nontheistic ethics as "relativism" is to make the assumption that we have access to truths from a source outside the human world. The ethical principles derived from human experience and intelligent reflection address the needs and interests of human beings living in a social world, and thus are relevant to the actual human situation. Humanists believe that what are claimed to be God-given rules are in fact the ethical principles of a particular group—such as ancient religious leaders, clergy, theologians, or church traditions—and reflect the particular biases of that person or group. Would the sexual ethics of Roman Catholicism be different, for example, if the clergy were not all male?

Similarly, since different cultures and religions have different sets of ethics, there can be no universal absolute ethic. Ironically, each system of "absolute" ethics is relative to its own culture.

The Possibility of Altruism

Can we ever put the interests of others ahead of our own, and if so is there a biological basis for such behavior? The primacy of self-centeredness discussed in the chapter on human nature raises the question of whether altruism is possible. As I have noted, even animals at the premoral stage exhibit some altruistic behavior, suggesting that some degree of altruism evolved over the hundreds of thousands of years of humankind's moral evolution. Sociobiologists have noted that cooperative behavior serves evolutionary purposes and thus is to some extent an inherited trait.

Zoologist Matt Ridley makes the case for a biological basis for altruism in his work *The Origins of Virtue*. He cites studies that show that our cooperative instincts may have evolved from our natural selfishness. Noting the paradox, he writes,

> Our minds have been built by selfish genes, but they have been built to be social, trustworthy and cooperative. . . . Human beings have social instincts. They come into the world equipped with predispositions to learn how to cooperate, to discriminate the trustworthy from the treacherous, to commit themselves to be trustworthy, to earn good reputations, to exchange goods and information, and to divide labor. . . . Far from being a universal feature of animal life, . . . this instinctive cooperativeness is the very hallmark of humanity and what sets us apart from other animals.

Since most people have high regard for those who do good for others, Ridley suggests that much altruistic behavior results from our desire to be well thought of. When others think well of us, we also feel good about ourselves. Some altruism, then, is motivated by enlightened self-interest.

Each of us could probably cite numerous examples of times when we have acted against our own self-interest or benefited from others' unselfish acts. Such acts by parents for their children are common, as are unselfish acts by members of larger family units for one another. But is altruism possible between total strangers?

One of the members of my former congregation, a humanist, volunteered to house refugees from El Salvador during that country's civil war. This woman, who lived alone, took the risk of opening her home to someone she had never met in order to protect him from deportation and certain imprisonment or death. When the refugee's wife was able to join him, she made room for her as well.

Some unselfish actions during World War II are well known. Raoul Wallenberg was a Swedish businessman who, due to Swedish neutrality, was able to travel throughout Germany and German-occupied countries during the war. When he became aware of what was happening to the Jews, he went to Budapest as a Swedish diplomat and issued "Swedish Protective Passes" to thousands of Jews to save them from deportation. Sometimes he stood between SS troops and a group of Jews, saying that if the troops wanted the Jews, they would have to shoot him first. As Soviet forces drew near, with bombs falling and intense fighting all around, Wallenberg remained in Budapest in order to protect as many Jews as possible. About 120 thousand Jews survived in Budapest, most of them because of Wallenberg, who lost his life, apparently at the hands of the Soviet secret police.

At least 1,200 Jews would have been killed had it not been for Oskar Schindler, who was no saint in many other ways but risked his own life to save them. Schindler, a German who had been an enthusiastic supporter of Nazism, operated a factory that made enamelware in occupied Krakow, Poland. Since the factory had been owned by Jews, many of the employees were Jewish. While the Nazis were herding the other Jews of Krakow onto the trains that would take them to Auschwitz, Schindler insisted that he needed his Jewish workers in his factory and that his factory was essential to the war effort. When necessary, he bribed the SS troops with his own money to save his Jewish workers.

Numerous ordinary German, Polish, Dutch, and Danish citizens housed or hid individual Jews or Jewish families, again at great risk to themselves. In this country, many people donate blood without knowing who will get it. Thousands of people have registered to donate their bone marrow if needed, again without knowing ahead of time who the recipient might be. These are some examples of altruism toward strangers.

Is altruism possible when considerable sacrifice is involved? Soldiers who give their lives for their country in time of war provide one example of such altruism. Many people support progressive causes, knowing that if those causes become policies they will have to pay higher taxes.

But, we must ask, are these examples simply illustrations of enlightened egoism? By supporting a cleaner environment, are we simply trying to make the planet a safer place for ourselves, our children, and our grandchildren? By giving money to Planned Parenthood, are we hoping to prevent a population explosion that would be harmful to ourselves or our offspring in the future? While there may be situations in which what appears to be altruism is enlightened self-interest, I doubt that egoism is the sole motivation, or even the primary motivation, in most instances of these kinds of actions. However, even if self-interest is involved to some degree, that does not negate the fact that what we are doing has beneficial consequences. People may give money to relieve hunger at least in part because it gives them a tax deduction and makes them feel better, but it is still a moral act because its results are salutary. One's motive does not have to be pure in order for an act to be ethical. Enlightened self-interest can and does lead to moral actions.

Rules or Consequences?

Traditionally ethical theory has been divided into two categories. Deontological ethics holds that obedience to rules is the essence of ethics and morality. In this view, it is the individual's task to obey the laws of some authority, such as nature or God. From this ethical perspective, the underlying concept of what it means to be human is submission and obedience. While much of religious ethics follows this perspective, humanistic religious naturalism does not.

An ethic of rules means that an act is always right or wrong regardless of the circumstances in which it is done. In this way of
thinking, if abortion is considered wrong, it is *always* wrong; there
is no situation in which it could be considered morally justifiable,
even if the pregnancy is due to rape or incest or if it threatens the
life of the mother. If lying is always wrong under all circumstances, it would be wrong for a person shielding a woman from
someone who wants to kill her to lie by telling him she is not
there. An ethic of rules followed strictly is not satisfactory.

A second type of ethical theory, the *teleological*, or consequentialist, viewpoint, starts not with rules but with the goal or conse-
quence of an action. Probably the best known theory of this type
is utilitarianism, which holds that moral acts are those which
achieve the greatest good for the greatest number of people. In the
teleological perspective, the essence of what it means to be human
is to be a creator of a better world.

Since the consequences of an act can vary in different situations, teleological ethics are situational. Thus, there may be some
situations in which lying is morally justifiable and others in which
it is wrong. The consequentialist shielding a woman, wanting to
save the woman's life, would swear to the would-be murderer that
the person he is seeking is not there. A consequentialist might regard abortion as morally justifiable in order to prevent an unwanted
child from being born or to safeguard the life of the mother.

A third type of ethics has been articulated only within the last
century: the ethics of responsibility. As articulated by Protestant
theologian H. Richard Niebuhr, it asks what is a fitting or appropriate response in any given situation. This type of ethic holds that
being human is to be in relationship with others and to acknowledge the claims of others upon us. We respond to the actions and
the needs of others, and our responses are governed by our interpretation of their actions. Because it emphasizes human relationships rather than abstract rights or rules, an ethic of responsibility
is more in keeping with the insights of feminist ethicists.

The feminist perspective offers an important corrective to

ethical theory which, having been dominated by men, has empha-sized rules, rights, and rationality. Carol Gilligan and others have noted that rather than relying on abstract rules of reason, women tend to be particularly concerned with personal relationships and with what those relationships require. The result is an ethic of care, in which the emotions play a larger role than reason. Rather than focusing on individual rights or duties, the women studied by Gilligan in her research into women's moral development were concerned about personal relationships and giving care to those for whom they felt responsible. The person following an ethic of responsibility would have to determine what response is the most fitting to promote the well-being of the other person. In the exam-ple of reproductive choice, this ethical stance asks what is the most appropriate response to a particular woman in her particular situ-ation. The person shielding another from a murderer would have to decide to whom he or she feels more responsible—the murderer or the person she is protecting.

An ethic of responsibility and care is not limited to personal ethics but applies as well to social ethics. In her study, Gilligan quotes a woman who says, "I have a very strong sense of being re-sponsible to the world, that I can't just live for my enjoyment, but just the fact of being in the world gives me an obligation to do what I can to make the world a better place to live in, no matter how small a scale that may be on."

Emotions

Making a decision using the ethic of responsibility, then, involves reflecting on our responsibility to others as well as attempting to anticipate the consequences of our possible actions. Using our fac-ulties of reasonableness and critical intelligence is certainly im-portant in ethical decision making. However, our emotions also play a central role.

As noted in the chapter "The Responsible Search for Truth," studies show that patients with damage to the emotional centers of the brain lack the ability to make moral decisions, despite the fact that otherwise their reasoning faculties are not affected. It appears that, although the choices we make depend on both our feelings and our reasoning working together, our emotions are the primary motivating factor in ethical decision making. I know, for example, that the outrage I feel when seeing or reading about injustice and oppression is the basis of my commitment to social justice work. My emotions arouse my interest and commitment; reflecting on how best to act enables me to decide what I can do. In his article "Humanist Morality in a Postmodern Age," Michael Werner tells us,

> There is literally a visceral response in a moral decision. Something evil makes our skin crawl. Protecting a helpless child elates us. Injustice leaves us with a "sick feeling in the stomach." The conscience is a physiological state that evolution has found to be useful in our genes' survival. The emotions reward or punish certain behaviors we now call moral. Our emotions, not rational decisions, motivate us.

It would seem that our moral feelings precede our moral principles, not vice versa, but both are important to the process of ethical decision making.

Free Choice

A basic assumption of humanist ethics is that human beings have genuine free choice in thinking and in making ethical decisions. We are able to make choices through reflection instead of through instinctive reactions. However, we do not have absolute freedom —freedom that is devoid of any genetic influence or cultural conditioning. Our freedom is relative and finite. Yet without some degree of freedom, there could be no ethical responsibility.

Much of what we think and do is implanted in our genes and comes from our evolutionary heritage. Much also represents what we learned from parents, teachers, and society in general. In a word, we are "programmed" to think and act in certain ways. But we can to some extent transcend this conditioning by reason and reflection. The more we develop our self-understanding and our ability to think critically, the less our behavior results from unreflective reactions and the more we can transcend our social and biological programming. Religious humanism has always disagreed radically with all deterministic philosophies and theologies. The view that God is omnipotent and omniscient negates human freedom by maintaining that God knows in advance what each person will do. If that is so, human beings have no real freedom. Religious humanism also differs from biological theories that claim all human action to be determined by our genetic inheritance and from sociobiology, which regards all actions as determined by a combination of biology and social conditioning.

Since human life is communal, freedom is never absolute in the sense that one's freedom is restrained by society. I am not free to cry "fire" in a crowded theater or to strike someone who said something I did not like. My freedom is constrained by my responsibility to others.

The nature of a society also affects the scope and extent of individual freedom. In a totalitarian society, the individual has little freedom. The possibility of freedom is greatest in a democratically organized society. Furthermore, the institutions within a society, such as the family and the workplace, must be democratic if they are to nurture and facilitate genuine freedom for each individual. In the words of the third Humanist Manifesto,

> Ethical values are derived from human need and interest as tested by experience. Humanists ground values in human welfare shaped by human circumstances, interests and concerns and extend to the global ecosystem and beyond. We are committed to treating each person as having inherent worth and dignity and to making informed choices in a context of freedom consonant with responsibility.

The Ethics of
Humanistic Religious Naturalism

I BELIEVE that *reverence for life* should be the basic ethical principle for humanistic religious naturalism. Reverence for life encompasses both personal and social ethics, and as Albert Schweitzer believed, it arises out of humankind's fundamental will to live, the evolutionary survival instinct. Since all living things possess the same will to live, our attitude toward all life should be respectful and reverential.

However, since all life also feeds on other life, each person must reflect on how to apply this principle. Most of us will create a hierarchy in which some forms of life are more precious than others. Thus we might justify eating plants but not animals, or some animals but not others. We might also object to the cruel treatment of animals bred only for consumption, to hunting birds and animals as a sport, or to the use of some animals in medical research. For a number of years, I served on a committee at the National Institutes of Health charged with reviewing research protocols dealing with animals. The committee had a very different attitude toward the use of monkeys than mice, for example. Approval of protocols depended on the degree of invasiveness or harm balanced with the anticipated benefit to humans.

Reverence for life underlines the sense of a mystic unity of all living things. Unitarian Universalist minister Richard Gilbert suggests its ethical ramifications: "Reverence for life gives rise to a moral imperative for love in interpersonal relationships, justice in social relationships and trusteeship in our relationships with our environment."

Love and Compassion

The Greek language has three words that can be translated as love. *Eros* refers to passionate desire, such as romantic love but also to love of learning or wisdom. *Philia* points to love between friends and family members; it can be rendered as brotherly or sisterly love. *Agape* connotes a more disinterested form of love, lacking the intensity of eros or the warmth of philia but with a connotation of acting for the well-being of others. Eros and philia are more emotional, while agape is usually understood as an act of will. Thus, when all three connotations of love are united, it means that love has both affective and volitional qualities. As Erich Fromm puts it, "Love is an activity, not a passive affect; it is a 'standing in,' not a 'falling for.'" Caring enough about a sick friend to take her to the doctor or visit her in the hospital is an act of love. So is tutoring an underprivileged child, volunteering in a low-income housing program, or working in a homeless shelter. I will never forget the love shown by several members of my former congregation toward a mother whose daughter was killed one afternoon. Upon learning of the death, I went immediately to the mother's home and found people already there, ministering to the broken-hearted woman. Love, then, can be described as an emotion that leads to action. Karen Armstrong notes that "compassion is the litmus test" for the religious ideas and doctrines of all the major religions of the world. If a belief leads to kindness, empathy, and generosity, it is good theology. If it does not lead to practical acts of love, it is bad theology. Armstrong adds that *compassion* does not mean pity or condescension, but "feeling with" another. M. Scott Peck defines love as "the will to extend one's self for the purpose of nurturing one's own and another's spiritual growth." His definition means that love has a goal or purpose: spiritual growth, meant in a very broad sense. Action seeking the well-being of another springs from respect for the other as a person of dignity and value. But Erich Fromm and others have shown that respect for others is possible only when one first loves and respects one's self. Self-love in this sense does not mean selfishness or self-centeredness; it simply refers to one's own sense of self-worth. Reverence for life includes reverence for one's own life.

Love is an expression of respect for persons. In ethical terms, this means treating all people as ends in themselves, not as means to one's own ends. In other words, we should not exploit or manipulate another person for our own purposes.

This principle can also be stated as the Golden Rule—to treat others as we would have them treat us, probably the most nearly universal ethical principle. In a word, an essential aspect of moral living is to put ourselves in the position of others before making a moral decision.

Sometimes we confuse loving and liking. The people we like are usually people with similar values and perspectives, or we may like them because of a particular quality or ability they have. But we may like a person without loving them—that is, without actively seeking their well-being—and we may love another person without especially liking them. Love requires effort and action.

In her experience as a Christian pastor, Rebecca Parker discovered a tragic misunderstanding of love in our society. Parker tells of women in her congregation who were abused by their husbands but did not report their abuse, believing that it was their Christian duty to suffer silently and without objection, as Jesus did. If a woman told her male minister about her abuse, she would most likely be told that her suffering brought her closer to Christ.

Parker also notes that the Christian story says that God the Father sent his son to suffer and die for the sins of the world, an act she refers to as "a pattern of divine child abuse." This sends three messages, she suggests: that unquestioning obedience is a virtue, that we should accept suffering and death in silence, and that self-sacrifice is a holy act. Parker then extends this to what she calls "the theology of war." She writes,

> Part of the mythos is that the young man, really the child, is expected by the fathers of the culture to give his life through military service, to be willing to make the ultimate sacrifice for the sake of love in order to redeem humanity. . . . I'd like to suggest that in this mythos we have a culture founded on the sacrifice of children.

This is not to say that the mythos of suffering and sacrifice is the only thing at work in either domestic violence or nationalistic militarism. Nevertheless, I find Parker's suggestions persuasive and powerful. I believe she has discovered something at work in the subconscious depths of our psyches that adversely affects both domestic and national life. A post-Christian humanistic ethic based on respect for persons—emphatically including self-respect—rejects this ethic of passive suffering and self-sacrifice.

Justice as Equity

Reverence for life applied to society takes the form of justice. We often define justice as giving everyone his or her due. But what is each human being due simply because he or she is human? Religious humanism maintains that all individuals are possessed of the same inherent worth and dignity. This means that a society should provide equal opportunities for all people—a more equitable distribution of resources and wealth and more equitable wages, educational opportunities, and housing. The huge disparity between rich and poor in this country cries out to be corrected. There is no moral justification for 20 percent of the population to have 85 percent of the wealth. For 1 percent of the population to have over 40 percent of the wealth is morally obscene. In a country where some people have annual incomes of seven figures while hundreds of thousands of children live in crowded substandard housing and go to bed hungry every night, something is terribly wrong. Nor is it just for some nations to have a per capita annual income of over $20,000 and others to have less than $500.

The 1986 pastoral letter by the Roman Catholic Bishops in the United States, entitled "Economic Justice for All" expresses a view that is consistent with humanistic naturalism:

> Distributive justice . . . calls for the establishment of a floor of material well-being on which all can stand. This is a duty of the whole of society and it creates particular obligations for those with greater resources. This duty calls into question extreme inequalities of income and consumption when so many lack basic necessities. Catholic social teaching . . . challenge[s] economic arrangements that leave large numbers of people impoverished. Further, it sees extreme inequality as a threat to the solidarity of the human community, for great disparities lead to deep social divisions and conflict.

Poverty means more than material deprivation. Poverty is dehumanizing because it undermines self-esteem and a person's sense of worth and dignity. Religious humanists can agree with the goals stated in the United Nations Universal Declaration of Human Rights:

> Everyone has a right to a standard of living adequate for the health and well-being of himself and of his family, including food, clothing, housing, and medical care and necessary social services, and the right to security in the event of unemployment, sickness, disability, widowhood, old age or other lack of livelihood in circumstances beyond his control.

As mainly middle- and upper-middle-class, highly educated people, liberal religionists tend to focus on issues of fairness and equity that concern the middle class, such as women's rights, gay rights, and the environment. We often fail to make our voices heard on issues that concern low-income and working-class people. One reason is that we remain untouched by the massive loss of working-class jobs to other nations and the failure of many

companies to provide benefits such as health insurance and retirement plans. Another reason for this neglect is probably that a
more equitable distribution of wealth might require some financial sacrifice on our part—through higher taxes, for example, or
increases in the costs of products as a result of higher wages. A few
years ago an essentially humanistic and socially active church
voted not to support a living wage bill that had been proposed in
the county legislature. It is important to transcend our own class
interests and extend our empathy to persons of other classes. Two
groups—the Unitarian Universalist Affordable Housing
Corporation, in the Washington-Baltimore area, and the nation-
wide Unitarian Universalists for a Just Economic Community—
give me hope that liberal religion can overcome its classism.

One of the basic reasons for the severe inequities in the United
States is that our values have been shaped by our Puritan legacy,
what historian Sydney Ahlstrom calls "the American's basic contempt for poverty." Economist R. H. Tawney writes,

> Convinced that character is all and circumstances nothing,
> [the Puritan] sees in the poverty of those who fall by the way,
> not a misfortune to be pitied and relieved, but a moral fail-
> ure to be condemned, and in riches, not an object of suspi-
> cion . . . but the blessing which rewards the triumph of
> energy and will . . . The moral self-sufficiency of the Puritan
> nerved his will, but it corroded his sense of social solidarity.

Unfortunately, many people in the United States still think
this way, even though the theological idea that prosperity is the reward of morality and poverty the wages of sin has been discred-
ited by mainstream theologians as well as by the biblical book of
Job and by Jesus (John 9:1–3). This idea is both sociologically in-
accurate and morally reprehensible, yet it continues to pervade
American society.

Justice as equity also includes equality between the sexes. As
long as women are not respected as much as men, and as long as
women are treated as less than equal to men in nearly every way,

no society can claim to be a just society. Although this issue has finally become a concern in modern society, women are still discriminated against in Europe and America, and much more so in Muslim countries. Unfortunately, the subservient role of women in the Western world stems in large part from Christianity and its negative view of sexuality. In the biblical story of creation, Eve is depicted as less important than Adam, and she is blamed for yielding to the tempter and thus bringing sin into the world. The apostle Paul had a very low regard for women, teaching that they should obey their husbands and remain quiet in church matters. By refusing to ordain women and discriminating against them in other ways, the Roman Catholic church has fostered and reinforced the oppression of women for two thousand years. The problem continues, particularly in evangelical Christianity, where the Bible is taken literally as the pronouncements of God rather than as writings that are relative to the culture and the time. Paul's admonition for wives to obey their husbands and his injunction against women speaking in church are cases in point.

The feminist movement has done much to close the equality gap between men and women. Still, women are paid less than men for essentially the same work, women's sports receive far less attention and financial support than men's, and many working women do much more of the housework than their husbands. Single mothers are one of the poorest demographics in the country, and a woman's right to abortion is continually threatened as more and more obstacles are erected to prevent the exercise of that right.

In American society, people of color and people with a same-sex orientation continue to be discriminated against as well. A larger percentage of African Americans are poor and poorly educated than the Euro-American population, the result of centuries of slavery and discrimination. Bisexual, gay, lesbian, and transgender people suffer from the prevalence of homophobia in our society. At a hearing on a bill in my state's legislature that would outlaw same-sex marriage and civil unions, the homophobic hate of those who favored the discriminatory bill was palpable in their emotional responses to the testimony. A humanistic religious naturalism committed to justice will oppose all forms of oppression —including discrimination based on social class, race, gender, or sexual orientation.

Justice as Freedom

With its emphasis on the development of human potential in each person, religious humanism has always considered freedom, understood as self-determinism, to be a central value. But individual freedom is limited by lack of education, economic poverty, and political tyranny. Freedom is greatest in truly democratic societies, but even within such societies, the poor and less well educated have fewer doors open to them than the more affluent and better educated. To seek justice, then, is to seek greater economic equity and better education, which are the *sine qua non* of political liberty.

True self-determination requires freedom from external authority. For the religious humanist, this includes being free from religious authorities and free to be one's own authority in religious matters. Self-determination includes being free to think and act for ourselves on social, economic, and political issues, as well as on issues of ethics and morality. But to be free is also to be responsible for what we say and do. Thus freedom carries with it not the burden of always being right—no one can claim that—but the burden of being honest, caring, and responsible. And to be responsible entails being informed and reflective about issues before making decisions, considering as many options as possible, and thinking critically about the viable alternatives.

Democracy

We usually think of democracy as referring to government of, by, and for the people. While that is true, the meaning and basis of democracy is the intrinsic value and dignity of each individual. Democracy is the only form of social organization that is consistent with the religious humanist understanding of both human dignity and human limitations. "Man's capacity for justice makes democracy possible," Reinhold Niebuhr suggests, "but man's inclination to injustice makes democracy necessary." Respect for the individual means that every organization and institution within a society, as well as every level of government, should follow democratic principles and practices. The humanist commitment to critical thinking rather than dogmatism can only flourish in a democratic framework, and only in a democratic society can there be a free exchange of opposing ideas without threat of retribution. Ideally, democracy both encourages the expression of different views and protects the rights of minorities. At its best, a democratic society can thrive as a pluralistic society.

Democracy in America today is gravely threatened by two groups, authoritarian religion and corporate interests. Proponents of the former seek to impose their conservative religious views on the nation by tearing down the wall of separation between church and state, which is an essential component of our freedom of speech and freedom of religion. They would have the government mandate prayer in the public schools, abolish reproductive rights, and finance some of their work. Corporate interests influence legislative policies through inordinate monetary contributions to political leaders. Legislators are beholden to companies whose lobbyists give them campaign money and expensive gifts. The policies lobbyists promote favor business interests and wealthy individuals and are generally adverse to both working-class and middle-class Americans. For example, the *Washington Post* reported that a group of companies, having paid $1.6 million to lobbyists, reaped the benefit of legislation that saved them over $100 billion (that is not a misprint) in tax savings! Poor and middle-class people will eventually have to pay more taxes as a result of this outrageous injustice.

Plutocracy—government by and on behalf of the wealthy— has replaced democracy as the American form of government. This has resulted in a sharp decrease in political liberty for the masses as well as the increasing disparity between the resources of the rich and the poor. A humanistic ethic rooted in equity and freedom mandates that its followers work for restoration of a truly democratic form of government—one in which the poorest voter has just as much power as the wealthiest, in which freedom in all areas and for everyone is increased rather than decreased, and in which true religious freedom is cherished and protected.

Political democracy is only one expression of the democratic principle. The foundation of democracy is respect for each individual and peaceful persuasion through the free exchange of ideas. Democracy encourages diversity and respect for minority views and opinions. In the sphere of economics, democracy means that each person has the right to a decent job with adequate wages, financial security, and a voice in economic policies. In social life, democracy means the abolition of social class and equal respect for all people, regardless of their place on the economic-educational ladder. In the realm of education, it means the right to attend good schools and equal opportunity to advance as far educationally as one's interests and ability permit. Culturally, democracy means the opportunity to develop an appreciation of the arts and literature and to enjoy these as one's interest and time allow. In voluntary associations and family life, it means empowerment of all members to participate in decision making. Genuine equality of the sexes would prevail in all areas, including the family.

Democracy is central to the humanistic vision of a world in which each person's value and dignity is honored.

Charity or Justice?

The kind of involvement of most churches and individuals who exercise social responsibility, such as staffing soup kitchens, working in homeless shelters, distributing food baskets at Thanksgiving, and giving children gifts at Christmas, is not so much social justice work as charitable activities. Much of the money given by caring people goes to charitable organizations that provide food, clothing, and shelter. Charity offers at least some temporary relief to people in need, and for that reason it is important, but it does not address the underlying problems that cause their suffering or oppression in the first place. That is the role of justice advocacy.

In a study of philanthropy entitled *Charity Begins at Home,* Teresa Odendahl concludes that the American system of philanthropy primarily serves not those in need but the affluent. She demonstrates that most of the charitable contributions of the very rich and the foundations they establish go to such institutions as Ivy League universities, art museums, and symphony orchestras. All of these enjoy the benefits of federal and state tax exemption, and they "exist primarily for the pleasure, edification and perpetuation of the upper classes." Even our system of philanthropy helps the haves much more than the have-nots.

Another problem with charity is that it relieves our consciences and enables us to feel that we have done something for others while not really sacrificing much. In short, it perpetuates a system that is good to those of us who belong to the middle and upper economic classes, but it does not result in fundamental or systemic change.

On the other hand, social justice work, with its emphasis on equality and freedom, is an effort to change unjust structures that cause inequality, suffering, and oppression. It takes the form of advocacy rather than charitable deeds. Advocacy requires patience, numbers, and often money in order to bring sufficient power to bear to change an unjust policy or practice. It does not often provide the immediate satisfaction of giving a helping hand to someone in need, but when it is successful, its long-term effects can be very significant.

Lessons from Liberation Theology

Religious humanists can learn much about justice from liberation theology. This Christian movement began in Latin America but includes groups within North America as well. Liberation theologians identify with oppressed and marginalized groups, especially the poor and racial or ethnic minorities. They believe that God advocates a "preferential option for the poor and oppressed" because these are the people who are in greatest need yet have the least power to change their situation.

Liberation theology is not simply concerned with raising poor and oppressed people's standard of living and level of education, important as these are. The main concern is that poverty and oppression are dehumanizing. The poor and oppressed are exploited; they suffer humiliation, rejection, defeat, and despair far more than others. In the words of Gustavo Gutierrez, one of the founders of liberation theology, "To be poor means to die of hunger, to be illiterate, to be exploited by others, not to know you are being exploited, not to know that you are a person."

Since religious humanism maintains the worth and dignity of all people, it follows that those who are poor, oppressed, powerless, and therefore dehumanized should receive particular consideration in matters of justice and equity. As in liberation theology, the goal is not only better education and living standards, but also the humanization that these things make possible.

A second aspect of liberation theology is a critique of the political and economic structures that result in poverty and oppression. To a large extent, poverty and oppression are the result of the way society is organized, including such matters as minimum wage laws, tax policies, racism and other discriminatory practices, and the delivery of health care. The task for liberation theologians—and for religious humanists—is to work to change the structures of society that keep people poor and oppressed, again with the goals of humanization and greater justice.

Humanistic religious naturalists need to overcome our class bias and work hard for policies aimed at improving the quality of life for the poor and oppressed. One example of this occurred in my home state, Maryland, when a number of us strongly supported the successful effort to get the state legislature to override the governor's veto of a bill requiring Wal-Mart and other large corporations in the state to provide health insurance for their employees.

The concept of justice as equity and freedom is of critical importance to the ethical principle of reverence for life. In its many aspects and ramifications it articulates reverence for life in human social existence.

Trusteeship

The damage to our natural environment caused by modern life has awakened our awareness that unless we change our thinking and our actions, life as we know it on this fragile planet will not survive indefinitely. Trusteeship is reverence for life applied to the natural environment. Its primary ethical principle is responsibility.

Western religion has played a significant role in our history of environmental exploitation. The God of the Hebrews was understood as a god who acted in history and, unlike the nature gods worshipped by their neighbors, was not concerned with nature. The God of the Hebrews led his people out of Egyptian captivity and later led them in wars against their enemies; he was a god who revealed himself primarily in human history. Christianity inherited this emphasis on humanity and this neglect of the sacred dimension of nature. Historian Lynn White famously suggested that the biblical injunction for humans to subdue the earth and have dominion over everything in it provided justification for the modern exploitation of the environment. The biblical emphasis on history rather than nature has led the Western world to develop science and technology. In doing so we have exploited nature's resources and polluted her air and water with the wastes of our factories and the exhausts of our trucks, airplanes, and automobiles. Nature was stripped of all sacredness and of all religious significance. The holy was to be found only in human actions and human history and in the supernatural.

An ethic of responsibility for the earth means that we must discard the idea that humans are dominant over nature and can do with it whatever we wish. This idea must be replaced with an attitude of respect and reverence toward nature and responsibility for its preservation. In doing this, we can learn from the Romantic poets, the Transcendentalists, and the Native Americans. These words, attributed to Chief Seattle, express the Native American view of the earth:

> Teach your children what we have taught our children—that the earth is our mother. Whatever befalls the earth befalls the sons and daughters of the earth. . . . The earth does not belong to us; we belong to the earth.

The United States has done a better job of reducing pollution than most other nations. Yet because of our wealth and our lifestyle, we are still one of the biggest polluters. Recent federal policies and practices have weakened or reversed much of our previous environmental progress. The battle to protect the environment is far from over; it is just beginning.

We are still filling the air with automobile and truck exhausts and the fumes from factories and power plants. Air pollution threatens our health and kills plant life. We are told that 20 percent of humans live in places where the air is unfit to breathe. When I visited Unitarian churches in Romania in 1993, the air in three of the cities was so bad that breathing it hurt my lungs and made me cough.

In the not-too-distant future, global warming caused by greenhouse gases will lead to elevated sea levels, floods, droughts, and loss of agricultural land and living space, causing catastrophic social and economic changes. Recently, winters in the Arctic have been so warm that polar bears are losing the floes they need for hunting. Seals are increasingly unable to find ice on which to bear their offspring and have to give birth on islands, where high tides can wash hundreds of the pups out to sea. Inuit people near the Arctic Circle complain about the heat. In early 2006, on days when the temperature would normally be twenty degrees below zero, it was forty degrees above. Diminishing ice in Greenland, Antarctica, and the Arctic adds to the evidence of global warming.

We are still pouring thousands of tons of industrial wastes into our rivers, polluting the waterways that we rely on for drinking water and recreation. Within a few years, it is almost certain that acute water shortages will affect large populated areas of the world because we are depleting water supplies faster than nature is able to replenish them. Desalinating ocean water is not yet a solution, since desalination plants use huge amounts of energy and create wastes that exacerbate environmental problems.

The land and its resources are also being depleted. Ecologists estimate that the present ecological footprint—the amount of land required to sustain human beings—already exceeds the actual land mass of the earth by nearly 20 percent. In the words of Loyal Rue, "Human beings are already exceeding the carrying capacity of the earth." This fact helps to explain the extent of malnutrition, starvation, and poverty. Food production is threatened by rapidly decreasing cropland. In the United States alone, an estimated 5,000 acres per day are lost as a result of topsoil erosion and the conversion of farmland to commercial and residential uses. By relying so heavily on fossil fuels, not only have we severely damaged our air and water but we are also rapidly exhausting the supply of oil, gas, and coal. We are cutting down trees for lumber and paper faster than we are replacing them. The tremendous biological diversity of the earth serves as a life support system for humankind, but biological species are disappearing more rapidly than new species are appearing. It is no exaggeration to say that there is a grave danger that within one hundred years or so, unless present practices change radically, the earth will not be inhabitable by any forms of animal or plant life.

In the ethic of trusteeship for nature, not only is polluting and ravishing the environment wrong but so is overpopulation, since it, too, threatens the fragile and intricate balance of life. At the present rate of population growth, there will be twelve billion people on the earth by the year 2025—far too many for the earth's resources to sustain. Thus birth control needs to be part of an environmental ethic.

Overproduction and overconsumption, too, are wrong, since they lead to the depletion of natural resources. Americans are ad-

dicted to consuming. We never have enough goods and products
to satisfy us, and our economy is said to depend on consumption.
Over 150 years ago, Emerson said, "Things are in the saddle and
they ride mankind." To curb consumption and protect natural resources, we must drastically reduce the use of fossil fuels. Reusing,
recycling, and safely disposing of toxic wastes all become moral
responsibilities.

The seventh Principle of the Unitarian Universalist Association is "respect for the interdependent web of all existence of
which we are a part." The web of life is indeed interdependent. If
one strand is broken or torn, the whole web is adversely affected.
Thus respect for all of nature is an essential part of an ethic of reverence for life. However, an ethic of trusteeship involves unpopu-
lar political decisions that are unlikely to be made without a
massive educational effort and changes in values.

By espousing a philosophy that affirms humankind as the primary value and regards it as superior to all other forms of life, the
humanist tradition has been complicit in this anthropocentric
perspective. However, humanistic naturalism, instead of thinking
of the natural environment as simply a resource for humans, regards all of nature as having intrinsic worth. Instead of positing
humankind as the lord of nature, humanistic naturalism sees us as
part of nature—not made up of a superior spiritual substance but
simply the most complex of all nature's creations. Humanistic
naturalism regards all of nature as sacred, so that protecting and
preserving the environment becomes a religious matter.

David Bumbaugh writes, "We are called to define the *religious*
and *spiritual* dimensions of the ecological crisis confronting the
world and to preach the gospel of a world in which each is part of
all, in which every place and every one is sacred, and every place is
holy ground, in which all are children of the same great love, all
embarked on the same journey, all destined for the same end."

Power to Effect Change

Institutionalized injustice can be changed only through the use of power. Religious people often think that power is evil, and so we do not trust it and are afraid to use it. But humanistic religious naturalists believe that power, like human nature, is neither good nor bad. It depends on how it is used. Martin Luther King Jr. said, "Power without love is reckless and abusive; love without power is sentimental and anemic." Each person is a center of power. Our task is to use our personal power on behalf of love and justice to effect systemic change.

One of the best ways to use power effectively is to form voluntary associations and coalitions of associations. Coalitions are important because there is strength in numbers. In today's world, groups that do not exercise their power on behalf of their interests and rights are usually left out of consideration by governmental or corporate entities. It was necessary for labor to organize in order to win better wages and conditions for working people. It was only when people of color, women, and gay people organized and advocated for their rights that the majority began to recognize those rights. Justice is won only when power is brought to bear against power. Having been involved with several groups that advocate for justice issues at the local and state levels, I would add that working together emphasizes our interdependence and social solidarity. It's also very personally rewarding. We can work with others who have different philosophical or theological views but who share the same social concerns.

Lawrence Kohlberg's highest level of moral development has to do with seeing ethical acts from the standpoint of their effects on humanity as a whole. Kant taught that one should act only on those principles that could be universally applicable. In making ethical decisions, it is important to see things from a global perspective, and to consider the future as well as the present. In the words of Peter Singer, "To live ethically is to think about things beyond one's own interests . . . . To live ethically is to look at the world with a broader perspective, and to act accordingly."

I believe reverence for life and its corollaries of love, justice, and trusteeship can be shown to be guiding principles that, if applied universally, would result in a far better world. Their application will differ from one culture to another and from one person's understanding to another's. But as general principles, I believe they represent the best of humanistic religious naturalism.

A Religion for the Future

I BELIEVE a viable religion of the twenty-first century must include at least five characteristics.

First is the affirmation that human beings are an integral part of nature. We are not separate and distinct from the rest of the natural world. We are related to every living creature, both plant and animal. The elements of which we are composed—carbon, calcium, iron—are the same elements of which the rest of the universe is made. We are not dominant over nature; we are its stewards and trustees.

The second characteristic follows from the first: A religion for the future will affirm humankind's responsibility to preserve and sustain the natural world.

Third, any viable future religion must take seriously the implications for religion of the remarkable discoveries of the modern natural and human sciences. The world of modern science is a different world from that of our ordinary perceptions and that of the ancient peoples who gave birth to Western religions. The religion of the future should be a religion that learns from science and adapts its teachings accordingly. And since every religion needs a story, the story of the religion of the future will be a scientific story with mythic significance.

Fourth, such a religion will recognize the importance of both reason and reverence. The human ability to think critically and constructively has made possible our many artistic achievements and medical and technological advances, but it is only reverence, understood as feelings of respect and awe, that can save us from the hubris that would destroy all the good we have accomplished. As Paul Woodruff writes in his elegant little book, *Reverence: Renewing a Forgotten Virtue*, "Reverence begins in a deep understanding of human limitations." And he goes on to note that reverence keeps human beings from acting like gods. It is thus essential to our true humanity. I also think a strong case can be made that lack of reverence is a major cause of all forms of human violence throughout history and in family and community life as well as with respect to the natural environment. And while reverence is not only a religious quality, a religion without a profound sense of reverence is no religion at all.

Finally, the religion of the future must affirm those values that help to make our lives more fully human. In her spiritual autobiography, *The Spiral Staircase*, religions scholar Karen Armstrong writes,

> In the course of my studies, I have discovered that the religious quest is not about discovering "the truth" or "the meaning of life," but about living as intensely as possible here and now. The idea is not to latch onto some superhuman personality or to "get to heaven" but to discover how to be fully human.

This is precisely what humanistic religious naturalism is all about. Becoming more fully human involves the transformation of the mind and heart from self-centeredness to a sense of one's self as part of a larger sacred whole and to a deep commitment to the human and natural worlds. It is about the transformation from a shallow life of fear, greed, hedonism, and materialism to a meaningful life of love and caring, gratitude and generosity, fairness and equity, joy and hope, and a profound respect for others.

By rejecting the idea of an afterlife, humanistic religious naturalism emphasizes the quality of life in this world. By eschewing dependence on supernatural powers, it empowers human beings to create lives that are joyful and meaningful here and now. By understanding human life as rooted and grounded in nature, it finds religious meaning and value in both the natural world and human community. With eyes open to the demonic side of human nature, it nevertheless retains a realistic hope for human progress and a better world.

Humanistic religious naturalism promotes an ethical life in which one thinks and acts from a larger perspective than one's own egoistic interests, a life that affirms the worth and dignity of each person, a life filled with wonder and reverence for the extraordinary magnificence of the natural world and human creations. It includes gratitude for the gift of life itself and the capacity to enjoy it.

To be fully human is to develop and use our minds but not neglect our emotions and intuitions. To me, it is a religious responsibility and a joyful challenge to learn all I can about human beings and the world in which we live and to think critically and constructively about what I learn. But we are also emotional beings who need to use our feelings in the service of the best that we know. A fully human person has both an open mind and a warm heart as well as a social conscience. As Bertrand Russell suggested, "The good life is one guided by reason and motivated by love."

The grounding of religious humanism in religious naturalism makes it possible to affirm a perspective that includes these five characteristics and thus qualifies as a religion for the twenty-first century. As the late Carl Sagan wrote, "A religion that stressed the magnificence of the universe as revealed by modern science might be able to draw forth reserves of reverence and awe hardly tapped by the conventional faiths. Sooner or later, such a religion will emerge." The religious perspective described in this book is just such a religion. I believe it is emerging among us today.

Notes

Introduction

p. xvii ...*at the center of our shared worldview.* Commission on Appraisal of the UUA, *Engaging Our Theological Diversity* (Boston: Unitarian Universalist Association, 2005), p. 92.

p. xx ...*significance of life.* Karen Armstrong, *A History of God* (New York: Ballantine Books, 1993), pp. 397–8.

Why I Am a Religious Humanist

p. 3 ...*and that I could see myself.* Fyodor Dostoevsky, *The Brothers Karamazov* (New York: Random House, 1950), p. 289.

p. 4 ...*children are put to torture.* Albert Camus, *The Plague* (New York: The Modern Library, 1948), pp. 196–7.

p. 5 ...*not satisfying to me.* For a fuller treatment of the theodicy problem, see William R. Murry, *A Faith for All Seasons: Liberal Religion and the Crises of Life* (Bethesda, MD: River Road Press, 1990), Chapter 6, "Why Do Bad Things Happen to Good People?"

p. 6 ...*temporarily imprisoned in a physical body.* Darwin recognized this as one of the implications of biological evolution, and that was one of the reasons he delayed publication of *The Origin of Species.* Many other scientists and philosophers concur, including Ursula Goodenough (see *The Sacred Depths of Nature*, Oxford: Oxford University Press, 1998, especially pp. 146ff.) and Chet Raymo (see *Skeptics and True Believers*, New York: Walker, 1998, pp. 245ff.)

p. 6 ...*to be persuasive.* Ludwig Feuerbach, *The Essence of Christianity* (New York: Harper Torchbooks, 1957).

p. 7 ...*a sign of alienation from others.* Sharon Welch, *A Feminist Ethic of Risk* (Minneapolis: Fortress Press, 2000), p. 111.

p. 9 ...*demanding interactions in the universe.* Stone, "Is God Emeritus?" *The Journal of Liberal Religion* 5, no. 1 (Spring 2005), http://meadville.edu/LL_JournalLR_v5n1_Stone.htm.

p. 10 ...*reality that connects us to all that is.* Andrew Newberg and Eugene D'Aquili, *Why God Won't Go Away* (New York: Ballantine Books, 2001), p. 9.

p. 10 ...*everyone and everything in existence.* Ibid., p. 2.

p. 10 ...*personal wholeness and social coherence.* Loyal Rue, *Religion Is Not About God* (New Brunswick, NJ: Rutgers University Press, 2005), p. 10.

The Religious Dimension

p. 14 ...*in accordance with this orientation.* Anthony Pinn, "On Becoming Humanist: A Personal Journey," *Religious Humanism* 32, nos. 1–2 (Winter/Spring 1996): p. 18

p. 15 ...*published as* A Common Faith. John Dewey, *A Common Faith* (New Haven, CT: Yale University Press, 1934).

p. 15 ...*religious in quality.* Ibid., p. 27.

p. 16 ...*through philosophical reflection.* Ibid., p. 14.

p. 17 ...*not primarily intellectual.* Ibid., pp. 20–1.

p. 18 ...*the devoutly religious men.* Albert Einstein, "What I Believe," quoted in Max Jammer, *Einstein and Religion* (Princeton, NJ: Princeton University Press, 1995), p. 72.

p. 19 ...*island in the sea of mystery.* Chet Raymo, *Skeptics and True Believers* (New York: Walker and Company, 1998), p. 47.

p. 19 ...*in complete astonishment.* W. MacNeile Dixon, *The Human Situation* (New York: Longmans, Green, 1937), p. 429.

p. 19 ...*that one thing was holy.* John Steinbeck, *The Grapes of Wrath* (New York: Viking Penguin Books, 1976), p. 105.

p. 20 ...*the movement of experience.* Dewey, *A Common Faith*, p. 37.

p. 21 ...*like an ever-flowing stream*. Amos 5:24. See also Micah 6:8: "What does the Lord require of you but to do justice, to love mercy, and to walk humbly with your God."

A Short History

p. 28 ...*obeisance to churches that promise eternal life*. Susan Jacoby, *Freethinkers: A History of Secularism* (New York: Metropolitan Books, 2004), p. 63.

p. 29 ...*establish systems incompatible therewith*. Ethan Allen, *Reason the Only Oracle of Man*, quoted in Jacoby, ibid., p. 18.

p. 29 ...*teachers of faith [into] expounders of nature*. Frances Wright, *Life, Letters, and Lectures*, quoted in Annie Laurie Gaylor, ed., *Women Without Superstition* (Madison, WI: Freedom from Religion Foundation, 1997), p. 43.

p. 29 ...*existences unseen and causes unknown*. Wright, ibid., p. 33.

p. 29 ...*profess what he does not believe*. Ernestine L. Rose, "A Defense of Atheism," quoted in Gaylor, *Women*, p. 84.

p. 30 ...*and promote his happiness*. Rose, ibid., p. 85.

p. 30 ...*and the magnitude of his works*. Elizabeth Cady Stanton, "The Ancient Polling Booth," quoted in Gaylor, *Women*, pp. 133–4.

p. 30 ...*Equality for all the children of the earth*. Elizabeth Cady Stanton, "Shall the World's Fair Be Closed on Sunday?" quoted in Gaylor, *Women*, p. 158.

p. 31 ...*the universe is all the God there is*. Roger E. Greeley, ed., *The Best of Robert Ingersoll* (Buffalo, NY: Prometheus Books, 1983), p. 34.

p. 31 ...*prayer dies upon the lips of faith*. Ibid, p. 81.

p. 32 ...*come to terms with 'the modern spirit'*. David Robinson, *The Unitarians and the Universalists* (Westport, CT: Greenwood Press, 1985), p. 209.

p. 32 ...*the Gospel of faith in man*. Francis Ellingwood Abbot, quoted in Charles H. Lyttle, *Freedom Moves West* (Boston: Beacon Press, 1952), p. 173.

p. 32 ...*in a new form—evolutionary naturalism*. Robinson, *Unitarians and Universalists*, p.108.

p. 35 ...*both the goodness and justice of God*. Daniel Payne, "Daniel Payne's Protestation of Slavery," quoted in Anthony Pinn, *By These*

Hands: A Documentary History of African American Humanism (New York: New York University Press, 2001), p. 28.

p. 35 ...*God does not exist.* Anthony Pinn, "On Becoming Humanist: A Personal Journey," *Religious Humanism* 32, nos. 1–2 Winter/Spring 1996: p. 15.

p. 35 ..."*We Choose Our Destiny.*" Mark Morrison-Reed, *Black Pioneers in a White Denomination* (Boston: Beacon Press, 1984), p. 134. The brief discussion of Lewis McGee is taken from the chapter on McGee in Morrison-Reed's book, pp. 113–40.

p. 36 ...*groups that oppress them.* William R. Jones, "Religious Humanism," in Pinn, *By These Hands*, p. 44.

p. 36 ...*any movement towards authentic freedom.* Ibid., p. 46.

p. 36 ..."*An African American Humanist Declaration.*" Norm Allen Jr., "An African American Humanist Declaration," in Pinn, *By These Hands*, pp. 319–26.

p. 36 ...*and Curtis Reese.* Much of the material in this and the next section is drawn from Mason Olds' excellent study, *American Religious Humanism* (Minneapolis: Fellowship of Religious Humanists, 1996).

p. 37 ...*whose favor they must curry.* Curtis Reese, *A Democratic View of Religion*, quoted in Olds, *American Religious Humanism*, p. 34.

p. 38 ...*the possibilities of all things.* John Dietrich, "The Religion of Experience," quoted in Olds, *American Religious Humanism*, p. 35.

p. 39 ...*we must accommodate ourselves.* John Dietrich, "Thankful—For What and to Whom?" quoted in Olds, *American Religious Humanism*, p. 69.

p. 39 ...*has made the individual what he is.* John Dietrich, "The Kind of Salvation Man Needs," quoted in Olds, *American Religious Humanism*, p. 81.

p. 39 ...*from the songs of the musicians.* John Dietrich, "The Immortal in Man," in *What if the World Went Humanist? Ten Sermons*, ed. Mason Olds (Yellow Springs, OH: The Fellowship of Religious Humanists, 1989), p. 96.

p. 41 ...*but not religiously necessary.* Curtis Reese, "The Dead Hand," quoted in Olds, *American Religious Humanism*, p. 41.

p. 41 ...*of his triumphant resurrection.* John Dietrich, "The Faith That Is In Us," quoted in Olds, *American Religious Humanism*, p. 42.

p. 42 ...*and make its way straight.* Olds, *American Religious Humanism*, p. 42.

p. 43 ...*effort to enrich human experience.* Curtis Reese, *Humanist Sermons*, quoted in Robinson, *Unitarians and Universalists*, p. 147.

p. 44 ...*to be able to meet those needs.* William F. Schulz, "Making the Manifesto," *Religious Humanism* 17 (Spring 1983): p. 89.

p. 44 ...*a candid and explicit humanism.* Paul Kurtz, ed., *Humanist Manifestos I and II* (Amherst, NY: Prometheus Books), p. 14. The Humanist Manifesto of 1933 can be found in many sources, including Corliss Lamont, *The Philosophy of Humanism* (Washington, DC: Humanist Press, 1997), pp. 311–5.

p. 46 ...*will be meditative.* Olds, *American Religious Humanism*, p. 23, paraphrasing Roy Wood Sellars, "Naturalistic Humanism" in *Living Schools of Religion*, ed. Virgilius Ferm (Patterson, NJ: Littlefield, Adams, 1965), p. 424.

Changes and Challenges

p. 50 ...*humanism as orthodoxy.* Richard Erhardt, "Beating a Cold Stiff Corpse," quoted in Frederic John Muir, "How We Got from There to Here: From Unitarian Christianity to Unitarian Religious Humanism," *Unitarian Universalist Selected Essays*, ed. Aaron Payson (Boston: Unitarian Universalist Ministers Association, 1999), p.120.

p. 53 ...*but for all of humankind.* Paul Kurtz, ed., *Humanist Manifestos I and II* (Amherst, NY: Prometheus Books, 1973), p. 14.

p. 53 ...*age or national origin.* Ibid., pp. 19–20.

p. 54 ...*a short prologue and epilogue. Humanism and Its Aspirations* (Washington, DC: American Humanist Association, 2003), www.americanhumanist.org/3/HumandItsAspirations.htm.

p. 56 ...*gives humankind ultimate freedom.* William R. Jones, "Theism and Religious Humanism: The Chasm Narrows," *The Christian Century* (May 21, 1975).

p. 56 ...*to religious humanism.* Rebecca Parker, "Vulnerable and Powerful: Humanism from a Feminist Perspective," *Religious Humanism* 27, no. 2 (Spring 1993): p. 55.

p. 57 ...*honest and loving.* For a more comprehensive religious humanist approach to pain and suffering, grief and loss, death and dying, see my book *A Faith for All Seasons* (Bethesda, MD: River Road Press, 1990).

p. 58 ...*as religious liberals.* Michael Werner, "Postmoderism and the Future of Humanism," in *Humanism and Postmodernism*, ed. Deborah

Shepard and Khoren Arisian (Minneapolis: North Amercian Committee on Humanism, 1994), p. 21.

Anchored in Nature

p. 62 ...*within a naturalistic framework.* Jerome Stone, "Is God Emeritus?" *The Journal of Liberal Religion* 5, no. 1 (Spring 2005), http://meadville.edu/LL_JournalLR_v5n1_Stone.htm.

p. 62 ...*their distinctive traits.* Donald Crosby, *A Religion of Nature* (Albany: State University of New York Press, 2002), p. 21.

p. 62 ...*the great living system.* John Ruskin Clark, *The Great Living System* (Boston: Skinner House, 1977).

p. 63 ...*are themselves natural events.* Rem Edwards, *Reason and Religion* (Lanham, MD: University Press of America, 1979), pp. 135–7.

p. 66 ...*open to their influence.* "Nature," *The Writings of Ralph Waldo Emerson,* ed. Brooks Atkinson (New York: The Modern Library, 1940), p. 5.

p. 66 ...*all mean egotism vanishes.* Ibid., p. 6.

p. 67 ...*transcendent self-understanding.* David Bumbaugh, "Toward a Humanist Vocabulary of Reverence," *Religious Humanism* 35, nos. 1–2 (2001): pp. 56–7.

p. 68 ...*becoming conscious of itself.* Julian Huxley, quoted in Amy Hassinger, "Welcome to the Ecozoic Era," *UU World* 20, no. 1 (Spring 2006): p. 28.

p. 70 ...*every other living being.* Brian Swimme and Thomas Berry, *The Universe Story* (San Francisco: Harper, 1992), p. 5.

p. 71 ...*anything but alone.* Ursula Goodenough, *The Sacred Depths of Nature* (Oxford: Oxford University Press, 1998), p. 78.

p. 72 ...*Of all my moral being.* William Wordsworth, "Lines," *A Treasury of Great Poems,* ed. Louis Untermeyer (New York: Simon and Schuster, 1942), p. 640.

Human Nature and Destiny

p. 75 *intense sympathy and strong hope.* William Ellery Channing, "Likeness to God," *William Ellery Channing: Selected Writings,* ed. David Robinson (New York: Paulist Press, 1985), p. 160.

p. 76 ...*sing that we live.* Robert Weston, "Out of the Stars," *Singing the Living Tradition* (Boston: Unitarian Universalist Association, 1993), no. 530.

p. 77 ...*three types of individualism.* Robert Bellah et al., *Habits of the Heart* (Berkeley: University of California Press, 1983), pp. 28 ff.

p. 80 ...*are increasingly irrelevant.* Bellah et al., *Habits of the Heart,* quoted in Peter Singer, *How Are We to Live?* (Amherst, NY: Prometheus Books, 1995), p. 32.

p. 80 ...*most individualistic nation in the world.* G. Hofstede, *Culture's Consequences* (Beverly Hills: Sage Publications, 1980), referenced in Singer, *How Are We to Live?* p. 32.

p. 82 ...*asked less of them.* Fyodor Dostoevsky, *Brothers Karamazov* (New York: Random House, 1950), pp. 304–5

p. 82 ...*cower to human opinion.* W. E. Channing, "Spiritual Freedom," quoted in *Singing the Living Tradition*, no. 592.

p. 86 ...*an imperial will-to-power.* Reinhold Niebuhr, *An Interpretation of Christian Ethics* (New York: Meridian Books, 1956), p. 110.

p. 86 ..."*see*" *others at all.* M. Scott Peck, *People of the Lie* (New York: Simon and Schuster, 1983), pp. 136–7.

p. 87 ...*middle of each human heart.* Richard S. Gilbert, *The Prophetic Imperative* (Boston: Skinner House Books, 2000), p. 73.

p. 90 ...*peace and beauty upon this earth.* Corliss Lamont, *The Philosophy of Humanism* (Washington, DC: Humanist Press, 1997), p. 15.

p. 91 ...*for eternal good or ill.* John Haynes Holmes, quoted in Gilbert, *Prophetic Imperative,* p. 56.

p. 92 ...*each is an integral member.* John Dietrich, "Can Human Nature Be Changed?" quoted in Mason Olds, *American Religious Humanism* (Minneapolis: Fellowship of Religious Humanists, 1996), p. 76.

p. 93 ...*who rest in unvisited tombs.* George Eliot, *Middlemarch* (New York: Bantam Books, 1985), p. 766.

p. 93 ...*riddle of the world.* Alexander Pope, "An Essay on Man," *A Treasury of Great Poems,* ed. Louis Untermeyer (New York: Simon and Schuster, 1942), p. 532.

p. 94 ...*with a spiritual soul.* Pope John Paul II, *Donum Vitae* ("Instruction on Respect for Human Life in its Origin and on the Dignity of Procreation"), The Vatican, 1987.

p. 94 ...*my forthcoming death.* Ursula Goodenough, *The Sacred Depths of Nature* (Oxford: Oxford University Press, 1998), p. 151.

p. 95 ...*the boundless sweep of being.* John Dietrich, "What I Believe," quoted in Olds, *American Religious Humanism*, p. 79.

p. 96 ...*undying music in the world.* George Eliot, "The Choir Invisible," *101 Famous Poems*, ed. Roy J. Cook (Chicago: Henry Regnery, 1958), pp. 137–8.

The Responsible Search for Truth

p. 98 ...*respectful of authority.* Chet Raymo, *Skeptics and True Believers* (New York: Walker), pp. 2–3.

p. 99 ...*external and nonrational pressures.* Rem Edwards, *Reason and Religion* (Lanham, MD: University Press of America), p. 379.

p. 100 ...*verify the solution adopted.* John Dewey, *How We Think* (Boston: DC Heath, 1910).

p. 101 ...*in human life.* Daniel Goleman, *Emotional Intelligence* (New York: Bantam Books, 1994), p. 4.

p. 102 ...*cost us our lives.* Ibid., pp. 8–9.

p. 102 ...*disabling—thought itself.* Ibid., p. 28.

p. 103 ...*recognize the injustice involved.* See Martha Nussbaum, *Upheavals of Thought: The Intelligence of Emotions* (Cambridge: Cambridge University Press, 2001).

p. 103 ...*the machinery of reason.* Antonio Damasio, *Descartes' Error: Emotion, Reason and the Human Brain* (New York: Harper Collins, 2000), pp. xii–xiii.

p. 103 ...*such a thing as passionate intelligence.* John Dewey, *A Common Faith* (New Haven, CT: Yale University Press), p. 79.

p. 104 ...*minds competing and interacting.* Michael Werner, "Humanism and Beyond the Truth" (unpublished paper, March 7, 1998), p. 3.

p. 105 ...*cultivation of feeling and love.* *Humanist Manifestos I and II* (Washington, DC: American Humanist Association, 1973), p. 18.

Feeding the Soul

p. 109 ...*a free and fearless response.* Henri Nouwen, *Reaching Out* (New York: Doubleday Image Books, 1986), pp. 50–1.

p. 109 ...*the world around us.* Sharon Welch, "Spirituality without God," *Tikkun* (May/June 1999): p. 69.

p. 111 ...*take hold of us.* Paul Tillich, "Address on the Occasion of the Opening of the New Galleries and Sculpture Garden of the Museum of Modern Art," quoted in Frank Burch Brown, *Religious Aesthetics* (Princeton, NJ: Princeton University Press, 1993), p. 91.

p. 113 ...*the* quality *of experience.* Jeaneane Fowler, *Humanism: Beliefs and Practices* (Brighton: Sussex Academic Press, 1999), pp. 50–1.

p. 114 ...*the very psalms of praise.* Richard Dawkins, "Is Science a Religion?" *The Humanist* 57, no. 1 (January/February 1997): www.2think.org/Richard_Dawkins_Is_Science_A_Religion.shtml

p. 114 ...*is surely spiritual.* Carl Sagan, *The Demon-Haunted World,* quoted in Jane Rzepka, "Science, Spirituality, Religion and All That," *Quest* 61, no. 8 (Sept. 2005): p. 2.

p. 114 ...*larger than one's own ego.* Parker Palmer, at Meadville Lombard Winter Institute (Madison, WI, February 2001).

p. 115 ...*when we face death.* C. G. Jung, *Modern Man in Search of a Soul* (New York: Harcourt, Brace and World, 1933), pp. 109–10.

Can We Be Good Without God?

p. 117 ...*because it is holy.* Socrates, quoted in Plato, *Euthyphro,* in *The Great Philosophers from Socrates to Turing,* ed. Ray Monk and Frederic Raphael (New York: Routledge, 2000), p. 24.

p. 118 ...*against Jews and blacks.* David M. Wulff, *Psychology of Religion,* quoted in Michael Shermer, *The Science of Good and Evil* (New York: Henry Holt, 2004), p. 236.

p. 118 ...*the war in Iraq.* Bill McKibben, "The Christian Paradox," *Harper's Magazine* (August 2005): online at www.harpers.org.

p. 119 ...*to ward off fishing boats.* See Michael Shermer, *The Science of Good and Evil* (New York: Henry Holt and Co., 2004) for a fuller account from an evolutionary perspective of how morality developed.

p. 120 ...*as in man.* Charles Darwin, *The Descent of Man,* quoted in Peter Singer, *Ethics* (Oxford: Oxford University Press, 1994), p. 44.

p. 120 ...*natural order of the universe.* E. O.Wilson, "The Biological Basis of Morality," *Atlantic Monthly* (April 1998): p. 58.

p. 120 ...*human population as a whole.* Ibid., p. 59.

p. 122 ...*the brotherhood of man.* Reuben Osborn, *Humanism and Moral Theory,* 2nd ed. (London: Pemberton Books, 1970), p. 85.

p. 123 ...*the social nature of man.* Basil Mitchell, *Morality: Religious and Secular* (Oxford: Clarendon Press, 1980), p. 139.

p. 124 ...*it greatly reinforces them.* John Ruskin Clark, *The Great Living System* (Boston: Skinner House Books, 1977), pp. 186–7.

p. 125 ...*culturally determined ethics.* Shermer, *Science of Good and Evil,* pp. 18–9.

p. 126 ...*apart from other animals.* Matt Ridley, *The Origins of Virtue* (London: Penguin Books, 1996), p. 249.

p. 130 ...*how small a scale that may be on.* Carol Gilligan, *In a Different Voice* (Cambridge, MA: Harvard University Press, 1982), p.19.

p. 131 ...*not rational decisions, motivate us.* Michael J. Werner, "Humanist Morality in a Postmodern Age," *Religious Humanism* 29, no. 3 (September 1995): p. 132.

p. 132 ...*freedom consonant with responsibility. Humanism and Its Aspirations* (Washington, DC: American Humanist Association, 2003).

The Ethics of Humanistic Religious Naturalism

p. 134 ...*relationships with our environment.* Richard Gilbert, *The Prophetic Imperative* (Boston: Skinner House Books, 2000), p. 90. I am indebted to Richard Gilbert for suggesting reverence for life as the basic principle of humanist ethics and to his outstanding book for some of the discussion which follows.

p. 134 ...*not a "falling for."* Rainer Funk ed., *The Erich Fromm Reader* (Atlantic Highlands, NJ: Humanities Press International, 1994), pp. 116–7.

p. 134 ... *"feeling with" another.* Karen Armstrong, *The Spiral Staircase* (New York: Alfred A. Knopf, 2004), pp. 290–3.

p. 134 ...*another's spiritual growth.* M. Scott Peck, *The Road Less Traveled* (New York: Simon and Schuster, 1978), p. 81.

p. 135 ...*divine child abuse.* Rebecca Parker, "Vulnerable and Powerful: Humanism from a Feminist Perspective," *Religious Humanism* 27, no. 2 (Spring 1993): p. 63.

p. 136 ...*the sacrifice of children.* Ibid., p. 65.

p. 137 ...*social divisions and conflict.* "Economic Justice for All: Pastoral Letter on Catholic Social Teaching and the U.S. Economy," quoted in

Richard S. Gilbert, *How Much Do We Deserve?* (Boston: Skinner House, 2001), p. 13.

p. 138 ...*his sense of social solidarity.* R. H. Tawney, *Religion and the Rise of Capitalism* (New York: Mentor Books, 1958), p. 191.

p. 141 ...*makes democracy necessary.* Reinhold Niebuhr, *The Children of Light and the Children of Darkness* (New York: Charles Scribner's Sons, 1944), p. xi.

p. 143 ...*of the upper classes.* Teresa Odendahl, *Charity Begins at Home* (New York: Basic Books, 1990), p. 36.

p. 144 ...*you are a person.* Gustavo Gutierrez, *A Theology of Liberation* (Maryknoll, NY: Orbis, 1973), p. 289.

p. 146 ...*we belong to the earth.* "Chief Seattle Speech Version 4," www.synaptic.bc.ca/ejournal/Seattle SpeechVersion4.htm.

p. 146 ...*forty degrees above.* "Inuit See Signs in Arctic Thaw," *The Washington Post* (March 22, 2006): p. A3.

p. 147 ...*carrying capacity of the earth.* Loyal Rue, *Religion Is Not About God* (New Brunswick, NJ: Rutgers University Press, 2005), p. 343. Much of the information in this paragraph comes from this book.

p. 148 ...*destined for the same end.* David Bumbaugh, "The Heart of a Faith for the Twenty-First Century," *Unitarian Universalism: Selected Essays* (Boston: Unitarian Universalist Ministers Association, 1994), p. 37.

p. 149 ...*to act accordingly.* Peter Singer, *How Are We to Live?* (Amherst, NY: Prometheus Books, 1995), pp. 174–5.

A Religion for the Future

p. 152 ...*of human limitations.* Paul Woodruff, *Reverence* (Oxford: Oxford University Press, 2001), p. 3.

p. 152 ...*to be fully human.* Karen Armstrong, *The Spiral Staircase* (New York: Alfred A. Knopf, 2004), pp. 270-1.

For Further Reading

Armstrong, Karen. *The Spiral Staircase*. New York and Toronto: Alfred A. Knopf, 2004.

Barlow, Connie. *Green Space, Green Time: The Way of Science*. New York: Springer-Verlag, 1997.

Bellah, Robert et al. *Habits of the Heart*. Berkeley: University of California Press, 1983

Bumbaugh, David, "Toward a Humanist Vocabulary of Reverence," *Religious Humanism*, vol. 35, nos. 1 and 2, 2001.

Clark, John Ruskin. *The Great Living System*. Boston: Skinner House Books, 1977.

Crosby, Donald. *A Religion of Nature*. Albany: State University of New York Press, 2002.

Damasio, Antonio. *Descartes' Error: Emotion, Reason and the Human Brain*. New York: HarperCollins, 2000.

Dewey, John. *A Common Faith*. New Haven, CT: Yale University Press, 1934.

Dietrich, John. *Ten Sermons*. Yellow Springs, OH: Fellowship of Religious Humanists, 1989.

Edwards, Rem. *Reason and Religion*. Lanham, MD: University Press of America, 1979.

Fowler, Jeaneane. *Humanism: Beliefs and Practices*. Brighton: Sussex Academic Press, 1999.

Fromm, Erich. *The Anatomy of Human Destructiveness.* Greenwich, CT: Fawcett Publications, 1973.

———. *The Heart of Man.* New York: Harper and Row, 1968.

Gaylor, Annie L. *Women Without Superstition.* Madison, WI: Freedom from Religion Foundation, 1997.

Gilbert, Richard S. *The Prophetic Imperative: Social Gospel in Theory and Practice.* Boston: Skinner House Books, 2000.

Goleman, Daniel. *Emotional Intelligence.* New York: Bantam Books, 1994.

Goodenough, Ursula. *The Sacred Depths of Nature.* Oxford: Oxford University Press, 1998.

Hassinger, Amy. "Welcome to the Ecozoic Era," *UU World,* vol. 20, no. 1, Spring 2006.

Humanist Manifesto III: "Humanism and Its Aspirations." Washington, DC: American Humanist Association, 2003. Available at www.american humanist.org

Huxley, Julian. *Evolutionary Humanism.* Buffalo, NY: Prometheus Books 1992.

Jacoby, Susan. *Freethinkers: A History of American Secularism.* New York: Henry Holt, 2004.

Jones, William R. "Theism and Religious Humanism: The Chasm Narrows," *The Christian Century,* May 21, 1975.

Lamont, Corliss. *The Philosophy of Humanism.* Washington, DC: Humanist Press, 1997.

Lyttle, Charles H. *Freedom Moves West.* Boston: Beacon Press, 1952.

Mitchell, Basil. *Morality: Religious and Secular.* Oxford: Clarendon Press, 1980.

Murry, William R. *A Faith for All Seasons: Liberal Religion and the Crises of Life.* Bethesda, MD: River Road Press, 1990.

Olds, Mason. *American Religious Humanism.* Minneapolis: Fellowship of Religious Humanists, 1996.

Osborn, Reuben. *Humanism and Moral Theory,* 2nd ed. London: Pemberton Books, 1970.

Nussbaum, Martha. *Upheavals of Thought: The Intelligence of Emotions.* Cambridge: Cambridge University Press, 2001.

Parker, Rebecca. "Vulnerable and Powerful: Humanism from a Feminist Perspective," *Religious Humanism*, vol. 27, no. 2, Spring 1993.

Persons, Stow. *Free Religion*. Boston: Beacon Press, 1963.

Pinn, Anthony. "On Becoming Humanist: A Personal Journey," *Religious Humanism*, vol. 32, nos. 1 and 2, Winter/Spring 1996.

———. *By These Hands: A Documentary History of African American Humanism*. New York: New York University Press, 2001.

Raymo, Chet. *Skeptics and True Believers*. New York: Walker, 1998.

Reese, Curtis W. *Humanist Sermons*. Chicago: Open Court Publishing Co., 1927.

Rockefeller, Steven. *John Dewey: Religious Faith and Democratic Humanism*. New York: Columbia University Press, 1991.

Ross, Warren R. "Confronting Evil," *UU World*, January/February 2002.

Rue, Loyal. *Religion is Not About God*. New Brunswick, NJ: Rutgers University Press, 2005.

———. *Everybody's Story*. Albany, NY: SUNY Press, 1999.

Sagan, Carl. *The Demon-Haunted World: Science as a Candle in the Dark*. New York: Random House, 1996.

Schulz, William F. *Making the Manifesto: The Birth of Religious Humanism*. Boston: Skinner House Books, 2002.

Shepherd, Deborah and Khoren Arisian, eds. *Humanism and Postmodernism*. Minneapolis: North American Committee for Humanism, 1994.

Shermer, Michael. *The Science of Good and Evil*. New York: Henry Holt and Company, 2004.

Stone, Jerome. "Is God Emeritus? The Idea of God Among Religious Naturalists," *The Journal of Liberal Religion*, vol. 5, no. 1, Spring 2005.

———. *The Minimalist Vision of Transcendence: A Naturalist Philosophy of Religion*. Albany: State University of New York Press, 1992.

Swimme, Brian and Thomas Berry. *The Universe Story*. San Francisco: Harper, 1992.

Turner, James. *Without God, Without Creed.* Baltimore, MD: The Johns Hopkins University Press, 1985.

Welch, Sharon. "Spirituality without God," *Tikkun,* May/June 1999.

———. *A Feminist Ethic of Risk.* Minneapolis: Fortress Press, 2000.

Werner, Michael J. "Humanist Morality in a Postmodern Age," *Religious Humanism,* vol. 29, no. 3, September 1995.

Wilson, E.O. "The Biological Basis of Morality," *Atlantic Monthly,* April 1998.

Woodruff, Paul. *Reverence.* Oxford: Oxford University Press, 2001.

Acknowledgments

I once asked a friend how long it had taken him to write his book. "All my life," he answered. I now understand what he meant because this book includes the odyssey, experiences, and relationships of a lifetime. That being said, certain people have been more directly influential. This book began when I was asked to present two lectures to the Florida Humanist Conference in March 2000. The chapters entitled "A Short History" and "Changes and Challenges" represent expanded versions of those lectures.

Two members of the Meadville Lombard Theological School faculty were particularly influential. David Bumbaugh's seminal essay, "Toward a Humanist Vocabulary of Reverence," stimulated my thinking as it has the thinking of many others. As I was seeking a foundation for a new humanism, Jerome Stone introduced me to religious naturalism, and that turned out to be decisive. Of course I am also indebted to many books by authors whom I know only through the writings cited.

I am also deeply indebted to Mary Benard, my editor at Skinner House Books, for making the book more readable and engaging, and to my wife, Barbara Murry, for reading and constructively critiquing the manuscript as well as for so much else during the forty-two plus years we have been together. I also appreciate the encouragement I received from the students in the course on religious humanism that I taught at Meadville Lombard. I am grateful for all the help I have received, but I alone am responsible for the book's weaknesses.

Index

United States
   contempt for poverty in, 138
   freethinking in, 28–31
   pollution in, 146
Universal Declaration of Human
   Rights, 137
*Upheavals of Thought: The
   Intelligence of Emotions*
   (Nussbaum), 102
Utilitarianism, 129
UU World, 51

Values. *See also* Ethical values;
   Morality
   beauty as, 112
   materialistic crisis in, 110
Vermeer, 111
Vishnu, 66

Walker, Alice, 119
Wallenberg, Raoul, 127
War, theology of, 136
Water pollution, 146–147
Wattleton, Faye, 119
"We Choose Our Destiny" (McGee),
   35
Wealth disparity, 136–137
Wealth redistribution, 138
Welch, Sharon, 7, 109
Werner, Michael, 58, 104, 131
Weston, Robert, 76
"What I Believe" (Einstein), 17–18
White, Lynn, 145
Whitman, Walt, 30
Why God Won't Go Away (Newberg
   & D'Aquili), 9–10
Wieman, Henry Nelson, 9, 34, 62
Wiesel, Elie, 4
Will to power, 87
Williams, David Rhys, 43
Wilson, Edward O., 120, 123
Wilson, Edwin H., 42, 43, 52
Wilson, James Q., 121
Women. *See also* Feminism
   in Christianity, 139
   equal rights for, 138–139
   in freethinker movement, 29
   moral development of, 130
   in patriarchal societies, 7–8

Women's movement, 56–57
Woodruff, Paul, 152
Wordsworth, William, 71–72
Wright, Frances, 29
Wulff, David, 118